A Study of Ezra Pound's Confucianism from the Modernization Perspective

现代化视野中的埃兹拉·庞德儒学研究

Tan Xiaocui

谭小翠　著

科学出版社

北　京

内 容 简 介

本书重点研究庞德视阈中的儒家思想。笔者首先从庞德与儒学研究的现状着手，追溯庞德与儒学相遇的历史语境、庞德皈依儒学的必然性；在此基础上，重点论述庞德的儒学观，解析他所理解的儒学对西方世界的影响。在庞德看来，儒家伦理是解决人与自己、人与社会、人与自然危机的有效方法，是医治西方社会根本“痼疾”的良药。

本书可供从事外国文学与儒学研究的科研人员、教师、学生阅读，亦可供喜爱外国文学与儒学的广大读者阅读。

图书在版编目（CIP）数据

现代化视野中的埃兹拉·庞德儒学研究=A Study of Ezra Pound's Confucianism from the Modernization Perspective 英文/谭小翠著. —北京：科学出版社，2020.4

ISBN 978-7-03-063645-4

Ⅰ. ①现… Ⅱ. ①谭… Ⅲ. ①庞德(Pound, Ezra 1885-1972)–儒学–研究 Ⅳ. ①B712.59 ②B222.05

中国版本图书馆 CIP 数据核字（2019）第 274036 号

责任编辑：杨 英 宋 丽 / 责任校对：贾娜娜

责任印制：李 彤 / 封面设计：蓝正设计

科学出版社 出版

北京东黄城根北街 16 号

邮政编码：100717

http://www.sciencep.com

北京虎彩文化传播有限公司 印刷

科学出版社发行 各地新华书店经销

*

2020 年 4 月第 一 版 开本：720 × 1000 B5

2020 年 4 月第一次印刷 印张：10 1/2

字数：220 000

定价：98.00 元

（如有印装质量问题，我社负责调换）

This work was aided by a grant from the Shandong Province Social Science Planning Research Program "A Study of Ezra Pound's Confucianism from the Modernization Perspective" (Project Number: 15CWXJ15).[①]

① 本书得到了山东省社会科学规划研究项目"现代化视野中的埃兹拉·庞德儒学研究"(15CWXJ15)资助。

Acknowledgements

I began the research when I was a postgraduate for my doctoral degree in 2011, and continued the study with a research grant from the Shandong Planning Office of Social Science. Additional grants from the Department of Education in Shandong Province and Qilu University of Technology have helped me defray the costs of the project.[①] For all the support, I am very grateful.

I feel deeply indebted to my mentor, Prof. Yootaek Sohn, who led me to Pound studies and encouraged my professional growth well beyond my graduate school years. To all professors at Suwon University, Republic of Korea, I'm grateful to them for the years of intellectual guidance and mentorship. My deep gratitude goes to Hyunsook Kim, Yongkwan Lee and Youngran Koh for their sustained encouragement and advice during the writing of my dissertation.

My special thanks go to Prof David Erben from University of Toledo, USA, who proofread the book and then wrote the preface. During the proofreading process, his academic spirit encouraged me to improve the book. Thanks also go to Prof Lauri Scheyer from Hunan Normal University, who supervised my study during my academic year at California State University, Los Angeles, USA. I'm grateful to those professors and scholars who have helped me in my very early academic years and have been encouraging my professional growth, including Hongxin Jiang from Hunan Normal University, Rong Ou from Hangzhou Normal University, Jun Liu from California State University, Los Angeles, Lianggong Luo from Central China Normal University, Zhuo Wang from Shandong Normal University, Baojie Li from Shandong University, Wenying Jiang from Queensland University, Australia. I also want to thank the outstanding scholars and my best friends Bai Liu, Jin Li, and Ping Hu.

---

① 本研究亦得到了山东省本科高校教学改革研究项目“基于对分模式(PAD)英语专业高年级核心课程课堂教学改革与实践”(M2018X073)和齐鲁工业大学“人文社科优秀青年学者支持计划”项目的资助。

I would like to thank my colleagues at Qilu University of Technology, who offered me help. Grateful acknowledgement is given to my editors, Ying Yang and Li Song of Science Press, for their especially warm and energetic roles. It has been a pleasure to work with Ning Zhang, my project editor. Finally, I must thank my husband and daughter who constantly supported and encouraged me to make the completion of the book possible.

Preface

Ezra Pound was born in October, 1885 in Idaho and died in November, 1972 in Italy. He was the son of Homer Loomis Pound and Isabel Weston Pound. His paternal grandfather, Thaddeus Coleman Pound, had worked dealing with railroads and lumber in Wisconsin. Phyllis Bottome described Pound's parents as:

> ... a quiet old fashioned and extremely pleasant type of American — common to our early childhood...[①]

Ezra Pound grew up in a comfortable middle-class home of the 1890s, and he entered the world of arts and humanities by enrolling at University of Pennsylvania as a non-degree-seeking student. Pound's friends during his time as a student included William Carlos Williams, who was studying medicine at the graduate school, and Hilda Doolittle, the daughter of professor Charles Doolittle at University of Pennsylvania. Hilda Doolittle, later known as the poet H. D., was a student at Bryn Mawr College.[②] Williams had been introduced to Pound by a student who remembered that Pound visited his dormitory room to read poems. Some of these poems appeared later in *A Lume Spento* (1908). Williams was also writing poetry.[③] "I was fascinated by the man," Williams wrote of Pound, "He was the liveliest, most intelligent and unexplainable thing I'd ever seen and the most fun except for his painful self-consciousness and his coughing laugh."[④] Throughout his life, Pound was a fierce supporter of his colleagues and friends.[⑤] In 1903 he enrolled in Hamilton

---

① Bottome, P. 1946. *From the Life*. London: Faber & Faber Ltd: 76.

② Stock, N. 1970. *The Life of Ezra Pound*. New York: Pantheon Books.

③ Williams, W. C. 1951. *The Autobiography of William Carlos Williams*. New York: Random House: 53.

④ Williams, W. C. 1951. *The Autobiography of William Carlos Williams*. New York: Random House: 58.

⑤ Hemingway wrote in 1925: "...Pound the major poet devoting, say, one fifth of his time to poetry. With the rest of his time he tries to advance the fortunes, both material and artistic, of his friends. He defends them when they are attacked, he gets them into magazines and out of jail. He loans them money. He sells their pictures. He arranges concerts for them. He writes articles about them. He introduces them to wealthy women. He gets publishers to take their books. He sits up all night with them when they claim to be dying and he witnesses their wills. He advances them hospital expenses and dissuades them from suicide. And in the end a few of them refrain from knifing him at the first opportunity." Qtd. in "Homage to Ezra", *This Quarter*, (1), Spring 1925: 221-225. In E. Hemingway, J. Matthew and J. S. Baughman (Eds.), 2006. *Hemingway and the Mechanism of Fame* (pp. 5-6). Columbia, SC: University of South Carolina Press.

College in New York. After graduation in 1905, he returned as a graduate student at University of Pennsylvania where he majored in English literature and romantic poetry. He was 21 when he graduated with an M.A. from University of Pennsylvania.[①]

As an American expatriate, Pound became a moving force in the avant-garde art scene in Europe, participating and influencing first the Imagist and then the Vorticist movements, and working closely with the poet T. S. Eliot among others. One of the most important developments in his career occurred when Pound came into possession of Ernest Fenellosa's notes on his (Fenellosa) translations of Chinese verse.[②] Pound's study of Fenellosa's translations helped him define and evolve his own poetic direction. His first free-verse translations of Chinese poetry were published in 1915 in *Cathay*, when he was 30. In *How I Began*, Pound wrote:

> I resolved that at thirty I would know more about poetry than any man living ... that I would know what was accounted poetry everywhere, what part of poetry was "indestructible", what part could *not be lost* by translation and — scarcely less important — what effects were obtainable in *one* language only and were utterly incapable of being translated.
>
> In this search I learned more or less of nine foreign languages, I read Oriental stuff in translations, I fought every University regulation and every professor who tried to make me learn anything except this, or who bothered me with "requirements for degrees."[③]

In pursuit of this ambition, he lived in London from 1908 to 1920, where he established a strong and often controversial reputation for himself as a leader of the literary avant-garde.[④] Through his criticism and translations, as well as in his own poetry, particularly in his *The Cantos,* Pound explored poetic traditions from different cultures ranging from ancient Greece, China, and the European Continent, to the contemporary UK and US.[⑤] He wrote to James Joyce in 1917: "I have begun an endless poem, of no known category...all about everything."[⑥] His cantos started

---

① Longenbach, J. 2009. Ezra Pound at home. *Southwest Review*, 94(2): 147-159.

② Fang, A. 1957. Fenollosa and Pound. *Harvard Journal of Asiatic Studies*, 20(1/2): 213-238.

③ Stock, N. 1964. *Poet in Exile*. Manchester: University of Manchester Press: 6.

④ Rainey, L. S. 1994. The creation of the avant-garde: F. T. Marinetti and Ezra Pound. *Modernism/Modernity*, 1(3): 195-220.

⑤ Slatin, M. 1963. A history of Pound's Cantos I-XVI, 1915-1925. *American Literature*, 35(2): 183-195.

⑥ Pound, E. 1966. Letter to James Joyce, March 17, 1917. In F. Read (Ed.), *Pound/Joyce: The Letters of Ezra Pound to James Joyce* (p. 102). New York: New Directions.

appearing in publications in the following years, and the *Draft of XVI Cantos* was published in 1925, followed by the *Draft of XXX Cantos* in 1930. The first commercial editions were published in 1933. More cantos were published between 1934 and 1940.①

In 1924 Pound moved to Italy. During this period in Italy, he became concerned with the economic reforms in the United States and the West.② He was also working on *The Cantos*.③ Pound also became increasingly involved in Italian Fascism, which he found to be a powerful agent for his own economic ideas.④ He made broadcasts in support of Mussolini's government on the Fascist radio in the 1940s, and in 1945 at the conclusion of World War II, he was arrested for treason by the United States. ⑤

Pound's anti-capitalism, and especially his economic ideas, are the intellectual source of both his embrace of Fascism and the anti-Semitic views that he expressed, both in poetry and prose (some of which he later, in a manner, recanted).⑥ Anti-capitalism for Pound derived from a very specific cultural convergence; late-19th-century Western culture, especially American culture, a culture where, as Pound experienced it and saw it, art was a decorative art and poetry had been turned into a commodity, subjected to the tastes of popular magazines and the public.⑦ This destroyed the potential for originality in art and subordinated art to money: usury in its

① Pound, E. Short biography. https://www.adnax.com/biogs/ep.htm [2018-10-28].

② Pound, E. 1939. *What Is Money For?* London: Greater Britain Publications; 1982. *What Is Money For? A Sane Man's Guide to Economics*. New York: Revisionist Press.

③ Barnes, D. 2011. Geographies of politics, geographies of literature: Ezra Pound and Italian modernism. *Comparative American Studies: An International Journal*, 9(2): 161-173.

④ Surette, L. 1999. *Pound in Purgatory: From Economic Radicalism to Anti-Semitism*. Urbana: University of Illinois Press.

⑤ Doob, L. W. 1978. Ezra Pound speaking: Radio speeches of World War II. Westport: Greenwood Pr.

⑥ "Allen explained how he tried to deal with anti-Semitic remarks. He said that he even got Ezra Pound to 'take it back,' to admit that it was a dumb, suburban prejudice." See, for example, Feldman, M. 2013. *Ezra Pound's Fascist Propaganda, 1935-1945*. Hampshire: Palgrave Macmillan; Casillo, R. 1983. Anti-semitism, castration, and usury in Ezra Pound. *Criticism*, 25(3): 239-265; Casillo, R. 1988. *The Genealogy of Demons: Anti-Semitism, Fascism, and the Myths of Ezra Pound*. Evanston: Northwestern University Press; Kashner, S. 2005. *When I Was Cool*. New York: Harper Collins Perennial.

⑦ See for example, Chace, W. M. 1970. Ezra Pound and the Marxist temptation. *American Quarterly*, 22(3): 714-725.

most horrifying, for Pound, sense.①

Pound's serious interest in Confucianism probably began in 1913 when Allen Upward, the author of *The Sayings of K'ung the Master* (1904), introduced him to Guillaume Pauthier's French translation of the Confucian work, *Les Quatre Livres de Philosophie Morale et Politique de la Chine* (1841).② In a letter to his wife, Dorothy Shakespear, dated 2 October 1913, Pound stated: "I'm stocked up with K'ung fu Tsze [Confucius], and Men Tsze [Mencius], etc. I suppose they'll keep me calm for a week or so."③ Pound's study of Confucian works (via Pauthier) led to the publication of his first article on Confucius in *The Egoist.* Entitled "The words of Ming Mao 'Least among the disciples of Kung-Fu-Tse'", the article underscores the importance Confucius places on self-cultivation. Indeed, Pound argued that this process was the "core" value in Confucianism.④

Pound's first original poetic creation based on Confucian works is Canto XIII, which explores the concept of self-cultivation extensively.⑤ In it, Pound used Pauthier's translations to synthesize and condense two of the four Confucian classics, *Da Xue* and *Lun Yu* (*The Analects*).⑥ In Canto XIII (58), the readers encounter a series of dialogues between Confucius and his students.⑦ Whenever Confucius asks a question, each of the students responds, and so a range of possible answers is proposed. One of the students, Zeng Xi, asks Confucius: "Which [student] had answered correctly?" Confucius replies: "They have all answered correctly, / That is to say, each in his nature." Significantly, Pound's translation changes the original text. In *Lun Yu* 11.25, Confucius judges his students' answers critically, favoring Zeng Xi's answer over the other students' responses.⑧ Pound eliminates Confucius's apparent

① Pound, E. 1960. *Impact: Essays on Ignorance and the Decline of American Civilization.* Chicago: Henry Regnery Company.

② Hakutani, Y. 1992. Ezra Pound, Yone Noguchi, and Imagism. *Modern Philology*, 90(1): 46-69.

③ Pound, E. 1984. *Ezra Pound and Dorothy Shakespear: Their Letters 1909-1914.* Ed. by O. Pound and A. Walton Litz. New York: New Directions.

④ Pound, E. 1914. The words of Ming Mao "Least among the disciples of Kung-Fu-Tse". *The Egoist*, 1(24): 456.

⑤ Jackson, T. H. 1974. The poetic politics of Ezra Pound. *Journal of Modern Literature*, 3(4): 987-1011.

⑥ Cheadle, M. P. 1989. The vision of light in Ezra Pound's *The Unwobbling Pivot. Twentieth Century Literature*, 35(2): 113-130.

⑦ Pevear, R. 1972. Notes on the cantos of Ezra Pound. *The Hudson Review*, 25(1): 51-70.

⑧ Kieschnick, J. 1992. Analects 12.1 and the commentarial tradition. *Journal of the American Oriental Society*, 112(4): 567-576.

preference, instead indicating that Confucius accepts *all* the answers equally. In doing so, Pound aligns this canto with ideas he had previously expressed in his essay "Provincialism the enemy" (1917). Here, as in Canto XIII, he maintains that Confucius respects the students' individuality and diversity even though the original text suggests otherwise. Hence, Canto XIII neither follows the traditional views on Confucianism nor aligns with critical studies on the ancient philosophy. Instead, Pound's interpretation of the ancient philosophy suggests that different ideas and discussions are valued in their own right.① In Pound's version, students are asked to reject the practice of following instructions in favor of thinking independently — a trait that Pound highly admires and promotes.②

Pound's interest in Confucianism deepened during the 1930s. In this decade, he began to learn Chinese so as to better understand the philosophical texts.③ During this process, Pound relied mainly on two sources: Robert Morrison's multivolume *A Dictionary of the Chinese Language* (1812) and James Legge's Chinese-English editions of the Confucian classics (1893).

Pound's promotion of Confucianism was closely associated with his efforts to promote Mussolini. Romano Bilenchi (1979: 435) observed that Pound once commented: "One day he explained to me that Fascist doctrine has its origin in Confucius, passed by way of Calvacanti, Flaubert, the German ethnologist Leo Frobenius and Enrico Pea directly to Mussolini, Hitler, and Oswald Mosley." For Pound, the modern embodiment of "proper conduct"④ was Benito Mussolini, who "as an ex-editor uses oratory" that deserves extensive examination.⑤ Mussolini's working experience as an editor in journals and newspapers had given him, in Pound's opinion,

---

① Huang, G. Y. 1993. Ezra Pound: (Mis)translation and (Re-)creation. *Paideuma: Modern and Contemporary Poetry and Poetics*, 22(1/2): 99-114.

② Zhu, C. G. 2006. Ezra Pound: The one-principle text. *Literature and Theology*, 20(4): 394-410.

③ Hoff, A. K. 2010. Language lessons: Pound's letters to his Chinese friends. *Journal of Modern Literature*, 33(2): 157-159.

④ "Proper conduct" or *zheng ming*. "For Confucius, *zheng ming* does not seem to refer to the 'rectification of names' (this is the way the term is most often translated by scholars of *The Analects*), but instead to rectify the behavior of people and the social reality so that they correspond to the language with which people identify themselves and describe their roles in society. Confucius believed that this sort of rectification had to begin at the very top of the government, because it was at the top that the discrepancy between names and actualities had originated." https://plato.stanford.edu/ entries/confucius/ [2018-08-17].

⑤ Pound, E. 1935. *Jefferson and/or Mussolini.* London: Stanley Nott: 65.

the ability to refine and enhance the texts he edited and reviewed.① He was responsible as an editor for ensuring the accuracy and effectiveness of the contents before publication.② Pound connected this editorial experience of Mussolini to a command of the written language and also to his public speeches, which, in Pound's opinion, were rhetorically well-composed and precise. Pound further emphasized that Mussolini was the only one who, for more than two decades, "has kept his word whereas it is almost impossible to find a public man in any other country, European or American whose promises are worth yesterday's newspaper"③.

The political significance, for Pound, of keeping the "word" signifies the principle and integrity of linguistic awareness. It also, problematically, reinforces an ideology of authoritarianism in which only persons in places of privilege and power can wield the power of language. Pound's praise of Mussolini was frequent and emotional, and he, unfortunately, had decided that the *II Duce* was a Confucian sage who should be acknowledged as the herald for a new and better age.④

According to the biographer David A. Moody, Pound intended to publish a series of Confucian texts in Italian as his founding contribution to Mussolini's Fascist Italy. He told the Italian Fascist journalist Fernando Mezzasoma: "I am absolutely convinced that in bringing to Italy a greater knowledge of the heroic doctrine of Confucius, I will bring you a gift of greater service than the Platonism that Gemisto brought you in the 14th century, which rendered you so great a service in stimulating the Renaissance."⑤

However, the war interrupted this project. While he was working on one of the Confucian classics, *Mencius*, as part of the project, Italian partisans arrived at his front door and arrested him for delivering pro-Fascist broadcasts from Rome.⑥ The *New York Times*, on May 6, 1945, carried the headline "EZRA POUND, WANTED FOR

---

① Nelis, J. 2007. Constructing Fascist identity: Benito Mussolini and the myth of Romanità. *The Classical World*, 100(4): 391-415.

② Dasenbrock, R. W. 1990. Ezra Pound, the last Ghibelline. *Journal of Modern Literature*, 16(4): 511-533.

③ Pound, E. 1935. *Jefferson and/or Mussolini*. London: Stanley Nott: viii.

④ Lauber, J. 1978. Pound's Cantos: A Fascist epic. *Journal of American Studies*, 12(1): 3-21.

⑤ Moody, D. A. 2015. *Ezra Pound: Poet — A Portrait of the Man and His Work*. Volume III. Oxford: Oxford University Press: 83.

⑥ Peterson, L. D. 1965. Ezra Pound: The use and abuse of history. *American Quarterly*, 17(1): 33-47.

TREASON, / Seized by American Forces NEAR Genoa in Italy".

After a psychiatric assessment, Pound was judged mentally incapable of standing trial.① He was sent to St. Elizabeths Hospital in Washington, D.C., where he remained until 1958.② Despite his confinement, Pound's energy was not diminished.③ He told Angela Palandri, a Chinese scholar who visited him at St. Elizabeths Hospital, of the impact of the bilingual edition of Confucian works that he had brought with him to Pisa:

> This little book has been my bible for years, the only thing I could hang onto during those hellish days at Pisa...Had it not been for this book, from which I drew my strength, I would really have gone insane.④

Pound's relentless energy and enthusiasm enabled him to continue correspondences with other writers, work on new sequences of "Rock Drills and Thrones" in *The Cantos,* and continue translating Confucian classics. It was also at this time during his hospital stay that he met the sinologist Achilles Fang (1910-1995), who offered assistance to Pound's exploration and knowledge of Confucianism.⑤

Pound's scholarship and an evaluation of the value of his creative works have gone through many phases, changes, and reevaluations over the years, both during his lifetime and after.⑥ His controversial fascination with Fascism, his support of Fascism, his anti-Semitism⑦, his emphasis on artistic individuality and his cross-cultural references have been the central issues addressed in many critical discussions of his works. Pound's works were, for the most part, ignored in the early 1900s, except by friends and colleagues like William Butler Yeats and T. S. Eliot. In this period, his challenging and experimental modernist style with its mix of languages and poetic

---

① Chace, W. M. 1987. Ezra Pound: "Insanity," "treason," and care. *Critical Inquiry*, 14(1): 134-141.

② History.com Editors. 2009-11-13. Federal court decides to release poet Ezra Pound from hospital for criminally insane. https://www.history.com/this-day-in-history/federal-court-decides-to-release-ezra-pound [2019-5-18].

③ Torrey, E. F. 1984. *The Roots of Treason and the Secrets of St Elizabeths*. New York: McGraw-Hill.

④ Palandri, A. 1974. Homage to a Confucian poet. *Paideuma*, 3(3): 301-311.

⑤ Hightower, J. R. 1997. Achilles Fang: In memoriam. *Monumenta Serica*, (45): 399-413.

⑥ Coyle, M. and Preda, R. 2018. *Ezra Pound and the Career of Modern Criticism: Professional Attention.* Boydell and Brewer: Camden House.

⑦ Taylor, C. H. 2010. Poetry, accountability and forgiveness: Ezra Pound and the Pisan cantos. *South Central Review*, 27(3): 104-132.

forms was not well-reviewed by literary critics. And, after the 1930s, Pound's works were, for the most part, condemned and overshadowed by his controversial political, economic and racial views and statements.① However, the importance of Pound's poetry started to be acknowledged with the publication of Hugh Kenner's influential work *The Pound Era* (1971). *The Pound Era* is a mixture of biographical and critical analyses of Pound's works with a focus on his epic, *The Cantos*.②

Pound's belief in Confucian principles has its roots in his statement: "It is the only system which shows a concern with social order."③ Pound devoted a lot of his time and energy to trying to translate the thoughts of Confucius into accessible language. In his translation entitled *Confucius: The Unwobbling Pivot and The Great Digest*, he wrote:

> Finding the precise word for the inarticulate heart's tone means not lying to oneself, as in the case of hating a bad smell or loving a beautiful person, also called respecting one's own nose. On this account, the real man has to look his heart in the eye even when he is alone.
>
> You improve the old homestead by material riches and irrigation; you enrich and irrigate the character by the process of looking straight into the heart and then acting on the results. Thus the mind becomes your palace and the body can be at ease; it is for this reason that the great gentleman must find the precise verbal expression for his inarticulate thoughts.
>
> One humane family can humanize a whole state; one courteous family can lift a whole state into courtesy; one grasping and perverse man can drive a nation into chaos. Such are the seeds of movement ... (semina motuum, the inner impulses of the tree).
>
> That is what we mean by: one word will ruin the business; one man can bring the state to an orderly course.④

Pound experienced an intellectual and creative awakening by reading Confucius, and he tried to apply what he learned in both his prose and poetry. Pound's Confucianism became an alternative to Western capitalism and modernity for him.⑤ Feng Lan concluded that Pound transformed Confucianism into a system for

① Beasley, R. 2007. *Ezra Pound and the Visual Culture*. Cambridge: Cambridge University Press.

② Kenner, H. 1971. *The Pound Era*. Berkeley: University of California Press.

③ Mullins, E. 1961. *This Difficult Individual*. New York: Fleet Publishing: 167.

④ Pound, E. 1951. *Confucius: The Unwobbling Pivot and The Great Digest*. New York: New Directions: 47.

⑤ Jung, H. Y. 1993. Confucianism as political philosophy: A postmodern perspective. *Human Studies*, 16(1/2): 213-230.

addressing many challenges inherent in the language, politics and religion of the modern Western world.① Through the philosophy of Confucius, Pound attempted to develop an alternative and new humanism, and use it to heal the social and political illnesses caused by the conflicts and failures he identified in the Western culture. Pound's interpretation of Confucianism led him to believe that an individual's moral will is the basis of truth and social order, and that the imperative for self-cultivation requires that a person fulfill his or her own social responsibilities through the active performance of Confucian virtues.②

Professor David Erben
University of Toledo

① "Lan's work is indispensable because of its comprehensive and astute arguments concerning Pound's engagement with Confucianism. Lan's study eliminates misconceptions frequently found in Pound studies, many of which tend to evaluate Confucianism as an archaic and authoritarian system of thought. By focusing on the direct study of Confucian works, Lan argues that Pound attained an impressive level of seriousness and depth when using Confucianism to engage issues confronting the modern world. His work also proficiently confronts the difficulties of presenting Confucius to readers of Pound." https://www.academia.edu/37556182/Ezra_Pounds_Translations_of_Confucius [2019-11-20].

② See Lan, F. 2005. *Ezra Pound and Confucianism: Remaking Humanism in the Face of Modernity*. Toronto: Toronto University Press.

Abbreviations

CEP	*Collected Early Poems of Ezra Pound*
Con	*Confucius: The Unwobbling Pivot, The Great Digest and The Analects*
EDP	*Ezra and Dorothy Pound: Letters in Captivity, 1945-1946*
EPCF	*Ezra Pound's Chinese Friends*
GB	*Gaudier-Brzeska: A Memoir*
GK	*Guide to Kulchur*
J/M	*Jefferson and/or Mussolini*
LE	*Literary Essays of Ezra Pound*
MAW	*Machine Art and Other Writings: The Lost Thought of the Italian Years*
PD	*Pavannes and Divagations*
SL	*The Selected Letters of Ezra Pound: 1907-1941*
SP	*Selected Prose, 1909-1965*
SR	*The Spirit of Romance*

A Note on Romanization and Chinese Characters

The *Hanyu pinyin* system is used through the book for Chinese names, dynasties and titles of Chinese works. Pound's romanization spellings of Chinese characters are preserved only in the quotations from his works, so as the traditional Chinese characters he cited.

Contents

Introduction

— Ezra Pound, Confucianism, and the Remaking of Western Humanism

This book examines Pound's attempt to use Confucianism as a cure for the West's "moral obtuseness". In doing so, it also examines the contributions of Pound's Confucianism to the West and to China. So this study focuses on three questions: First, what's Pound's Confucianism? Second, is the disordered West remedied by Pound's Confucian prescription? Third, in what way does Pound's Confucianism contribute to the modern world?

To answer these questions, the book also examined previous studies on Pound's Confucianism. To date, the most extended research on Pound's Confucianism is Feng Lan's *Ezra Pound and Confucianism — Remaking Humanism in the Face of Modernity* (2005). The work has made a very valuable contribution by systematically studying Pound's Confucianism in the fields of language, politics and spiritual beliefs. Another important work is Mary P. Cheadle's *Ezra Pound's Confucian Translations* (1997) in which Cheadle elucidates many issues concerning Pound's translation of Confucian classics and the influence of Pound's translations on his poetry. Her investigation, however, is largely limited to Pound's Confucian translations due to her inability to use source-language materials. And the last book that is worth mentioning is the work of a Chinese scholar, Jinmei Suo's *Confucianism in Pound's The Cantos* (索金梅, 2003), which has demonstrated that Pound's Confucian paradise is the major theme of *The Cantos*. Though some argumentation in her book looks less persuasive, the Confucian principles summarized by the author are inspiring.

Because of his works and papers concerned with Pound's Confucianism, Lan (2005: 3) is now considered to be the leading Poundian Confucian scholar. This book expounds on Pound's involvement in Confucianism and divides Pound's dealings with Confucianism into three phases: imitative, creative and comprehensive. Lan's article "Ezra Pound's etymographic reading and his interpretation of Confucian texts" (2001) traces Pound's etymographic interpretation with Confucian texts, and presents the damage Pound's interpretation has done both to the Chinese language and the Confucian texts. But the article also points out that by using this method, Pound believed he could "supersede previous Confucian translators and produce his own Confucius" (Lan, 2001: 26). Another article "Ezra Pound/Ming Mao: A liberal disciple of Confucius" argues that Pound is a liberal disciple in his early contact with Confucianism (Lan, 2004: 79).

The study of Pound's Confucianism is prosperous and productive in Poundian scholarship. Yao-hsin Chang (常耀信, 1988: 131) completely denied Pound's Confucian translations. He argued: "His (Pound's) rendition of the Confucian prose works is a failure…we cannot take Pound's version of the 'Four Books' seriously as a work introducing the thought system of Confucius." But Hugh Kenner (1985: 312) considered Pound's *Confucius: The Unwobbling Pivot and The Great Digest* as a "creative work of a high order" and simply called it "one of Pound's most important poems". Marianne Moore (Qtd. in Gordon, 1988: 149) also spoke highly of the same book and she regarded it as the "high thing" that can "supplant life".

Achilles Fang (1954: xiii) hailed Pound as "a Confucian poet"①, and Angela Palandri (1974: 301) paid "homage to the (a) Confucian poet". In her article, Palandri, with deep feelings, recalled her first contact with Ezra Pound and two memorable visits among her frequent ones to St. Elizabeths Hospital, Washington, D. C. where Pound was confined. The dialogues between Pound and Palandri during her first visit to St. Elizabeths Hospital have provided scholars with a lot of quotations. Among them, the most highly-cited one is as follows:

> "This little book has been my bible for years," remarked Pound, "the only thing I could hang onto during those hellish days at Pisa…Had it not been for this book, from which I drew my strength, I would really have gone insane…so you see how I am indebted to Kung."② (Palandri, 1974: 305)

John J. Nolde's book *Blossoms from the East: The China Cantos of Ezra Pound* (1983: 25) studies Pound's "China Cantos" which are based on de Mailla's *Histoire de la China*. Nolde's essay "Ezra Pound and the 'Ta Hio'" (1986: 73) puts forward four inspiring questions: "What was the Ta Hio? How did EP (Ezra Pound) discover it? What did this small Confucian classic mean to him? How did he try to use it?" At the same time, it provides reasonable answers and finally even compares Pound to "the

① Achilles Fang states that "Pound now emerges as a Confucian poet" in the introduction to Pound's *Shih-Ching: The Classic Anthology Defined by Confucius* (Cambridge: Harvard University Press. 1954: xiii).

② "This little book" refers to the pirated and bilingual edition of James Legge's translation of the "Four Books" of Confucius. Pound put it into his pocket when he was taken away by two Italian partisans on 3 May, 1945.

illustrious King Wen" and Ssu-Ma Ch'ien (Sima Qian 司马迁) (Nolde, 1986: 91). Moody's "*The Pisan Cantos*: Making cosmos in the wreckage of Europe" (1982: 137) argues "what Mussolini had meant to Pound" is "the will toward order" and what makes *The Pisan Cantos* new is that "the effort has become an intensely and urgently personal affair" and Pound's attempt himself to make cosmos in his own immediate little world (Moody, 1982: 140). Cayley's "Ch'eng, or sincerity" (1984: 203) relates *cheng* 诚, one of the central Confucian virtues, to "Pound's sincerity as an art critic, a sincerity which derives from the practice of the 'serious artist'".

Songping Jin's "Observation of natural scenes: Ta Hsser and Pound's later cantos" discusses the Neo-Confucian concept of Kê wu (*ge wu* 格物) and connects it to Pound's ideogrammic thinking and virtues (*de* 德) from heaven, or the heavenly order in the later cantos, especially focusing on the poetic lines of natural scenes (Jin, 1994: 7). Burton Hatlen's "Pound and nature: A reading of canto XXIII" (1996: 161) argues that there are three general meanings of "nature" for Pound — "nature as a system of powers", "nature as 'NOUS, the ineffable crystal'" and "nature as a play of physical and chemical processes", and examines how these conceptions of nature "shape the form and content of *The Cantos*".

Scott Eastham's essay "In Pound's China — the stone books speak" (2004: 109) systematically discusses the influence of "the stone books" on Pound, which analyzes it in three aspects: "Gateway to China — Vortex Venice", "Stone Books Speak — Symbol ≠ Sign", and "Three Worlds — Making it New". Eastham (2004: 109) argued in the last section that Pound had found "what may best be called 'sacred secularity'" in the Chinese "three worlds" of heaven, man, and earth. Additional introductions to Cheadle and Lan are necessary because they also have written articles on Pound's involvement with Confucianism in addition to their book-length works. Cheadle's "The vision of light in Ezra Pound's *The Unwobbling Pivot*" (1989: 113) holds that Pound "merges a totalitarian interpretation of Confucianism with a metaphysical, Neoplatonic vision of light" in order to "disentangle his Confucianism from the fascism with which he had allied it". Moreover, the essay also discusses the evolution of Pound's Confucianism, his idea of "totalitarianism" and his interest in Neoplatonism. Nobody can ignore Cheadle's contribution to the study of Pound's Confucianism. But as for this essay, it's hard for the author of the book to agree with her on Pound's purpose of merging Confucianism with a Neoplatonic vision of light. Pound merged the vision of light in his Confucian translation of *The Unwobbling Pivot* with a Neoplatonic vision of light because he found a similarity between them, and there's no obvious penchant for "disentangling his Confucianism from the fascism". Cheadle's book *Ezra Pound's Confucian Translations* is the first "extended study" on Pound's Confucianism (Lan, 2005: 7). The work has made a great contribution to Pound's translation of Confucian classics, the relevance of Pound's Confucian translations and his poetry writing. However, as for a study of translation, her inability in source-language confined her understanding of the implicit meanings of Pound's Confucian versions.

Qingjun Li's "Ezra Pound's poetic mirror and the 'China Cantos': The healing of the West" sets a good example for the healing function of Confucianism to the West. He argued: "Pound used poetry as his medium to mirror those Confucian values that he felt were indispensable for the healing of Western civilization and culture." (Li, 2008: 41) But his analysis was just confined to Canto XIII and Cantos LIII, LV, and LVI from the "China Cantos". Chungeng Zhu's (2005, 2006) two articles, centering on a holistic analysis of Pound's Confucianism and his poetic form, are "Ezra Pound's Confucianism" and "Ezra Pound: The one-principle text". The former specifically examined the relationship between Pound's Confucianism and his poetic form in presenting Jefferson and Adams, and the latter examined how Pound applied his Confucianism as a unifying method in *The Cantos*. Peter Makin (2005) argued, in his "Pound, Confucian sincerity, and America", that Pound's Confucian sincerity represented by *cheng* 诚 is what American literature lacks. These previous studies offer great inspiration for the present study — a systematic study of Pound's Confucianism to heal the Western society and to influence the modern East.

Since the 1950s, a great number of Ph.D. students in the West have focused on Pound's relationship with China, and chosen it as the subject of their dissertations. Many of the dissertations have later been published and became important source materials for Pound studies, such as Achilles Fang's, Cheadle's, Lan's and so on. Some excellent dissertations still remain unpublished. William Shu-sam Tay's dissertation *The Sun on the Silk: Ezra Pound and Confucianism* (1977) is the earliest "book-length" comment on Pound's Confucianism. It considers the ideogrammic method as a prefiguration of Confucianism, the personal order as the precondition of a larger order, the abundance of nature as Pound's linking Chinese rites with those of the Eleusinian mysteries, Confucianism as leitmotif in *The Pisan Cantos*, and finally history as poetry by focusing on Canto XIII, Cantos LII-LXII, *The Pisan Cantos* and "Section: Rock-Drill". Alan Lawrence Kelley Jr.'s dissertation *Confucianism and the Meaning of The Cantos of Ezra Pound* (1986) maintains that it's Confucianism that unifies *The Cantos* and this is proved with examples of Confucian heroes, Confucian conscience, etc.

In the 21st century, Zhaoming Qian has made a special contribution to the study of Pound's Confucianism. He has a good command of English and Chinese languages and knows both Chinese and English cultures well. He has written both in English and in Chinese, and he's always able to provide thoughts provoking insights in his writing. His three books, *Orientalism and Modernism: The Legacy of China in Pound and Williams* (Qian, 1995), *The Modernist Response to Chinese Art: Pound, Moore, Stevens* (Qian, 2003b), and *East-West Exchange and Late Modernism — Williams, Moore, Pound* (Qian, 2017), argue more or less the influence of Confucianism on Pound's poetic writing, although they do not specifically engage Pound's Confucianism. His article "Ezra Pound and his first Chinese contact for and against Confucianism" recalls Pound's early contact with Confucianism, and proves the significance of Pound's initial Confucian exploration which "gave birth to convictions later to become firmly embedded in Pound's Confucianism" (Qian, 2006: 167). His edited work *Ezra Pound and China* (2003) is a great contribution to Pound scholarship. Several papers on Pound's Confucianism in this collection are fantastically inspiring, including Hong Sun's "Pound's quest for Confucian ideals: The Chinese history cantos" (2003) and Wendy Stallard Flory's "Confucius against confusion: Ezra Pound and the Catholic chaplain at Pisa" (2003). The latter recalls Pound's contact with the Catholic chaplain Father Van at Pisa. It also includes Ronald Bush's "Confucius erased: The missing ideograms in *The Pisan Cantos*" (2003). Qian's *Ezra Pound's Chinese Friends: Stories in Letters* (2008) collects Pound's correspondence with his Chinese friends, which is another valuable contribution to Pound studies and has become a source that scholars reference when they study Pound's relationship with China. Qian is also very active in Chinese academic circles. He has many Chinese publications in China, which will be discussed later.

The study of the relationship between Pound and Confucianism started in the 1980s in China. A few research articles were published during this time. Entering the 21st century, it has been growing in popularity. Numerous academic papers have been published, and a couple of books centering on the relationship of Pound and Chinese culture have been published. Especially in the second decade of the 21st century, studies about Pound in China are becoming more and more popular in a variety of academic fields. These newly-published books have paved the way for a comprehensive study of Pound's works. Hongxin Jiang's book *Ezra Pound Studies* (蒋

洪新, 2014) is "a milestone for Chinese researches on Ezra Pound" and it offers "a brief history of Pound's life, a collection of Pound's poems in Chinese translation, a list of Pound's works, and a summary of previous researches on Pound in China and abroad" (谭小翠, 2015: 154). As the first comprehensive study on Pound, it provides Chinese scholars with a panoramic view of Pound and Pound studies. Besides, Jiang and Li edited *Ezra Pound: A Collection of Criticism* (蒋洪新, 李春长, 2014) which contains the Chinese translations of 23 articles covering Pound's life, poetics, translations and political ideas. He's also published dozens of papers on Pound poetic and translation theories. Indeed, his years of study on Pound have contributed a lot to Chinese Pound studies.

It remains to be seen how many more books and articles will be introduced and interpreted by Chinese scholars. Some scholars maintain that Pound is a Confucian poet, and his poetic theory and poetic writing are influenced by Confucianism. Perhaps the first one who discussed this issue in China was Feng Lan. He held that Confucius's *zheng ming* (正名) influences Pound's poetic theory, i.e. the "precision" of the poetic language (蓝峰, 1984). Peiwen Chang's "Ezra Pound: A messager of Chinese culture" recalls the history of Pound's involvement with Chinese culture and the Confucian influence on his writings (常沛文, 1986). Jian Mao's "Confucius on stilts: Ezra Pound and Chinese classical culture" argues that Pound sets up his paradise on Confucian doctrines (冒键, 2001). Zhengshuan Li and Wei Sun (李正栓, 孙蔚, 2011: 65) argued in their article "Ezra Pound's reception of classical Chinese poetry and philosophy" that Pound's later writing is obviously influenced by traditional Chinese painting, and the "order" Pound learned from Confucius is "the corner stone of a harmonious society, which also became the very foundation of his poetical and ethical ideas". Yige Zhu's "On Confucian affinities of Ezra Pound's poetics and their presentation in *The Cantos*" holds that Confucian doctrines of "gradation of order" and "right naming" are manifested in *The Cantos*, and "right naming" inspires "Pound's thinking over the function of language" and becomes "one of the sources of Pound's poetics of modernism" (朱伊革, 2012: 117).

Naikan Tao's *Pound and Chinese Culture* is one of the most valuable works on how Chinese culture, especially Confucianism, influenced Pound's poetic writing (陶乃侃, 2006). It focuses on Pound's reception of Confucian doctrines and ethics as well as Pound's reception of traditional Chinese poetics. It starts from Pound's comparative poetics, then the Chinoiserie and *Cathay*, to the three cantos (Canto I–Canto III) and Canto IV, and finally to Canto XIII and Canto XLIX, depicting Pound's involvement with Confucianism and its role in *The Cantos*. Qiyao Wu's *Ezra Pound and the Chinese Culture: Also on the Role of Foreign Literature on the Modernization of Chinese Culture* traces the Chinese elements in Pound's *Cathay* and the whole cantos (吴其尧, 2006). It argues that Pound has made two breakthroughs in culture. Pound regarded Eastern culture or Chinese culture as a complementary part of Western culture, and he made this first breakthrough in the process of learning and borrowing Chinese characters and classic poetry. And then Pound made his second breakthrough by turning to nature to pursue a self-purified cultural resource, and absorbed Confucian ideas on politics and economics as well as morals into his writing. Xiaocui Tan's two papers mainly focus on Pound's deep involvement with Confucianism: "Ezra Pound's conversion to Confucianism" presents how and why Pound turns to Confucianism and argues that Pound has already got the essence of Confucianism in his early studies of Confucian classics (Tan, 2014); "Consistency (one-principle) in Ezra Pound and Confucianism" argues Pound's life-long embracing of Confucianism (谭小翠, 2015: 24-29).

There are also scholars who have focused on the role Pound's Chinese friends played in his Confucian translations and the poetic writing of *The Cantos*. Zhaoming Qian and Rong Ou made important contributions in this field. Scholars from Hangzhou Normal University published a series of articles on Pound's contact with his Chinese friends and finally made them into a book *Ezra Pound Among Chinese Talents* (钱兆明, 2015), which is a very valuable book that became a source for Pound's Confucian studies. It includes eight chapters①: "Pound's encounter with Faxiang Song"②, "The *Seven Lake Canto* — The collaboration of Ezra Pound and Baosun Zeng"③, "Politicization of Confucianism: Debate and friendship between Ezra Pound and Fengqi Yang"④, "Achilles Fang: A Chinese friend and Pound's late translation of Confucian cantos"⑤, "As Confucius had it — The debate between Carsun

① Each chapter has been published as an independent article. There're small variations when the articles came into a book. The following eight footnotes (including this one) offer published information of each article.

② 钱兆明, 管南异. 2011. 逆向而行——庞德与宋发祥的邂逅和撞击. 外国文学, (6): 122-131.

③ 钱兆明, 欧荣. 2012.《七湖诗章》：庞德与曾宝荪的合作奇缘. 中国比较文学, (1): 90-101.

④ 钱兆明, 陈礼珍. 2014. 兼听则明：庞德和杨风岐的儒学政治化争论与情谊. 杭州师范大学学报（社会科学版), (1): 101-107.

⑤ 钱兆明, 欧荣. 2015. 缘起缘落：方志彤与庞德后期儒家经典翻译考. 浙江大学学报（人文社会科学版), 45(3): 124-132.

Chang and Ezra Pound"①, "Ezra Pound's collaboration with David Wang"②, "Ezra Pound's collaboration with Tze-chiang Chao"③, and "Exploration of Naxi Rites in Ezra Pound's late *Cantos*".④ Though each chapter has been published as an independent article, Qian has made an effort to organize them into a comprehensive book, including an inspiring 21-page preface. Additionally, Rong Ou has also made a research on Pound's interest in an official of Qing Dynasty, namely Youpu Wang (王又朴), and explored Pound's use of *The Sacred Edict* in *Thrones de Los Cantares* (欧荣, 2013a: 72-85).

Confucian works by Chinese scholars in *The Cantos* have also been published. Besides Jinmei Suo's book *Confucianism in Pound's Cantos* (索金梅, 2003), other scholars have mainly centered their researches on Confucianism in Pound's later cantos. Yiheng Zhao's "Ezra Pound the Confucianist — China in his later *The Cantos*" emphasizes that "Confucian culture not only brought new blood to *The Cantos* but also deeply influenced Pound's world outlook and views of history", and holds that "Pound attempted to establish a post-war new European world with Confucian ideology" (赵毅衡, 1996: 42). Zhao later developed his idea in his book *The Wandering Muse: How China Changed American Modern Poetry* (赵毅衡, 2003). Guiming Wang's "Confucianism in *The Pisan Cantos*" discusses the Confucian paragraphs in the "Four Books" that Pound wrote and the characters Pound used in the poetry. It argues that it's Confucianism that makes *The Pisan Cantos* more philosophical and poetical (王贵明, 2001a: 87). Wang also discussed Pound's adoption of Chinese characters in another article, namely "The temptation of Chinese diagrams and the spirit of Ezra Pound's *The Cantos*", and held that Pound "intended to present a symphony of the Western and Chinese cultures" by "the profound connotations and the artistic make-ups of the Chinese diagrams" (王贵明, 2001b: 41).

Ping Hu's "On Pound's poetic Confucianism in *The Pisan Cantos*" maintains that Pound enriched *The Pisan Cantos* with Confucian fragments by "carefully selecting some fragments of Confucianism, making necessary changes to meet different

① 钱兆明, 陈礼珍. 2015. 还儒归孔——张君劢和庞德的分歧与暗合. 中国比较文学, (3): 152-166.

② 钱兆明, 欧荣. 2014. 《马典》无"燊": 庞德与江南才子王燊甫的合作探源. 外国文学研究, (2): 48-56.

③ 钱兆明, 管南异. 2014. 《管子》"西游记"——赵自强和庞德《诗章》中的《管子》. 中国比较文学, (2): 114-126.

④ 钱兆明, 叶蕾. 2013. 庞德纳西诗篇的渊源和内涵. 中国比较文学, (3): 83-95.

emotional and aesthetic needs, and integrating them into his thinking, consciousness and creation" (胡平, 2013: 123). Hu also developed his thoughts on Confucianism in *The Pisan Cantos* in his book *A Study of Ezra Pound's The Pisan Cantos* (胡平, 2017). Wang and Chen (王伟均, 陈义华, 2017: 38) analyzed the visualization of Confucian-culture in *The Cantos*, which is mainly reflected in three aspects: the ideographic function of Chinese characters, the refinement of the syntax structure from Chinese classical poetry, and the juxtaposition and presentation of Confucian-culture visual scenario and events.

Canto XLIX, well known as the "Seven Lakes Canto", has attracted numerous scholars' interests since its publication in 1937. Hongxin Jiang's "Ezra Pound's 'Seven Lakes Canto' and Xiaoxiang Eight Views" explores how Pound wrote the poem and how Pound's theories of translation and poetics are reflected in the cantos (蒋洪新, 2006: 31). There are hot debates about the gist of the poem. Naikan Tao argued that the Xiaoxiang Eight Views present the aesthetics of Chinese landscape poetry and Confucian ethics (陶乃侃, 2006)①, while William Yip and Zhaoming Qian held that this canto conveyed the Taoist principles of tranquility and peace (叶维廉, 2008; Qian, 2003b). Rong Ou studied the implied theme of the canto and argued that it's a perfect combination of the aesthetics of Taoism and the political ideals of Confucianism (欧荣, 2013b: 229).

Hong Sun's "On Ezra Pound's *The Cantos* and Confucian classics" expounds that *The Cantos* looks disorderly and unsystematic, but everything is clear if one reads it from the perspective of Chinese culture, because it's the order of *The Great Learning* (*Da Xue*) that gives the long epic order. What's more, Chinese history in *The Cantos* provides the order, and Chinese characters provide detailed illustrations to it (孙宏, 1999). Years later, Hong Sun published another essay "From a name-giver to a 'one-man university': Tracing Pound's poetic discourse", which considers that Pound was a terrorist. He argued: "In the latter stage, while under custody, he (Pound) had to rely on his disciples in his 'Ezuversity' as his substitution to carry out terrorist undertakings, whereas he himself controlled them in remote secrecy." (孙宏, 2017: 23)

---

① Tao made a detailed study of Canto XIII and Canto XLIX in his book *Pound and Chinese Culture* and maintained that Canto XIII is the overt presentation of Confucian ethical theme and Canto XLIX is the covert one in *The Cantos*.

It's clear to see the sharp turn of Sun's attitude towards Pound. Although there're different voices about Pound's appropriation of Chinese culture, Sun's opinion is the most radical among them.

Other scholars have researched the relationship between Confucianism and Neo-Platonism in Pound. Ping Hu's "Projecting and blending: Neo-Platonism and Confucianism in *The Pisan Cantos* by Ezra Pound" argues that Pound blends Confucianism with Neo-Platonism in *The Pisan Cantos* through their two core concepts (order and virtue) and some classical images such as light and water (胡平, 2015: 2). Xiaochun Song's "Neo-Platonism vision of light and Pound's translation of *Zhong Yong* (*The Unwobbling Pivot*)" argues that Pound's translation of *Zhong Yong* contains philosophical ideas of Neo-Platonism vision of light. It argues that *Zhong Yong* and Neo-Platonism share some similarities of the mystical and transcendental "the One" and a hierarchical construction "realized through the readjustment of *Zhong Yong*'s structure, the adaptation of Neoplatonism's statements and the analysis of the formation of Chinese characters" so as to lift "*Zhong Yong*'s philosophical profoundness" and diversify "its acceptance in the Western countries" (宋晓春, 2014: 127).

As for Pound's translations, a hot debate exists in his translations of Chinese classical poetry, such as his *Cathay*. As for his Confucian translations, they are not as controversial as the poetry translations in the field of translation study. But it's still aroused scholars' interest in exploring his Confucian translations. Lan (2005: 8) argued that Pound is "known to Chinese cultural comparatists mostly as a major English translator of Chinese poetry; few of them are aware of Pound's hand in promoting a Western understanding of Confucianism".

As a matter of fact, Pound's Confucian translations are getting more and more attention within the field of translation study. Besides the studies of Pound's versions, such as Xiaochun Song's "Neo-Platonism vision of light and Pound's translation of *Zhong Yong* (*The Unwobbling Pivot*)" (宋晓春, 2014), there're also comparative studies of different versions of the "Four Books". Ping Yang's "Creative translation and cultural appropriation — on Pound's Confucian translations" holds that Pound translates Confucian classics in order to convey his own political ideal and provide a prescription for a corrupt Western society thus rewriting and appropriating Confucius results in misreading and distortion of Confucianism as well as Chinese culture as a whole (杨平, 2010). In his book *A Cross-cultural Study of the English Translation of The Analects*, Yang treated Pound as a sinologist and compared his version of *The Analects* with those of Arthur Waley, Simon Leys and Roger T. Ames & Henry Rosemont, Jr. (杨平, 2011). Hui Wang's "A comparison of Confucian *The Analects* translated by James Legge and Ezra Pound" compares the two versions in terms of the purpose of translation, the interpretive approach and linguistic features so as to produce a highly idiosyncratic translation of *The Analects* (王辉, 2004: 140).

There're also some studies centering on Pound's theory of translation. Hongxin Jiang (蒋洪新, 2001: 77) is one of the pioneering scholars who study Pound's achievements in translation, the theory of translation and the influence of translation upon his writings. Jianxin Zhou (周建新, 2011: 156) maintained: "Pound's translation is an unfaithful translation from both the views of translating and beautiful creation with regard to artistic creation." Chaowei Zhu (祝朝伟, 2006) and Yige Zhu (朱伊革, 2007) compared the translations of Pound and Lin Shu. Both of them regarded the translations of Pound and Lin as creative ones, and valued the positive effects of their translations.

Regarding Pound's enthusiasm for Chinese culture, there are two voices in China. An academic debate is worth mentioning. Xinlian Liu's "Understanding or misunderstanding? — Reconsidering the relationship of Ezra Pound and China" argues that Pound takes advantage of Chinese culture to carry his ideal, cure the illness of the Western society and save him from the mental crisis (刘心莲, 2001). Guiming Wang refuted her ideas via the article "Pound and Chinese culture — Discussing with the author of 'Understanding or misunderstanding? — Reconsidering the relationship of Ezra Pound and Chinese culture'" (王贵明, 2003). Qing Wang and Hongchuan Dong (王庆, 董洪川, 2018: 97) fully affirmed the efforts Pound has made in the modernist poetic revolution and maintained that what Pound has done creatively in his writing is "for the purpose of changing the world". They asserted that Pound's aesthetic revolution is "cultural salvation". Such an argument is really fresh. However, it's not the final judgment, and the study of Pound and Chinese culture is far from being exhausted.

To study Pound's Confucianism associated with modernization has a great significance in two fields: Poundian scholarship and Confucian scholarship.① As for the first field, so far, studies on Pound's Confucianism, as shown above, have made progress since the 21st century. However, except for the above-mentioned works, there have been few long systematic discussions with special relevance to Pound's Confucianism although some major critical works on Pound, such as Hugh Kenner's *The Pound Era* (1971), Donald Davie's *Ezra Pound* (1982) and Michael A. Bernstein's *The Tale of the Tribe: Ezra Pound and the Modern Verse Epic* (1980), have touched upon the topic more or less. The second field of Confucian scholarship is particularly concerned with the 20th-century New Confucianism.② Since the 1980s, some New Confucian believers, like Weiming Tu (杜维明)③ and Chung-Ying Cheng (成中英)④ have been engaging in studying modern values of Confucianism in both Eastern and Western societies and making endeavors to establish a bridge and facilitate better communication between the East and the West through Confucianism.

Pound's Confucianism, basically speaking, is about Confucian ethics through which Pound intended to save the disordered Occidental world. Being organized into three parts in addition to an introduction and a conclusion, the book consists of seven chapters: 1) Pound and Confucius: A Historical Confrontation; 2) Pound's Conversion to Confucianism; 3) Pound's Ideas on Man and Self; 4) Pound's Ethics on Man and Society; 5) Pound's Ethics on Man and Nature; 6) Pound's Confucianism as a Remedy for Western Disease; 7) The Legacy of Pound's Confucianism. Part I (Chapters 1-2) offers the historical background when Pound advocated Confucianism; Part II (Chapters 3-5), based on the close reading of Pound's essays, letters, prose, poetry

---

① See a detailed discussion in Chapter 7 "The Legacy of Pound's Confucianism" of the book.

② Feng Lan is the first scholar who connected Pound's Confucianism with the 20th-century New Confucianism (*xiandai xin rujia* 现代新儒家). See Feng Lan's book *Ezra Pound and Confucianism — Remaking Humanism in the Face of Modernity* (2005: 196-198). Qingjun Li also offered inspiring remarks on this topic in his essay "Ezra Pound's poetic mirror and the 'China Cantos': The healing of the West" (2008: 52).

③ Weiming Tu (Du Weiming, born in 1940) is one of the most famous Chinese Confucian thinkers of the 20th and 21st centuries. As a prominent member of the third generation of "New Confucians," Tu stressed the significance of religiosity within Confucianism. He wrote many works on Confucianism, such as *Confucian Thought: Selfhood as Creative Transformation* (Albany: State University of New York Press, 1985). See https://www.iep.utm.edu/tu-weimi/.

④ Chung-Ying Cheng (Cheng Zhongying, born in 1935) is a distinguished scholar of Chinese philosophy. He is considered as one of the pioneers who formalized the field of Chinese philosophy in the United States in the 1960s. he wrote books on Confuciansim, such as *A Treatise on Confucian Philosophy: The Way of Uniting the Outer and the Inner* (Beijing: China Social Sciences Publishers, 2001). See https://en.wikipedia.org/wiki/Chung-ying_Cheng.

(such as *The Cantos*), and Pound's Confucian translations, systematically analyzes Pound's Confucianism; Part III (Chapters 6-7) explores Pound's Confucianism and the modern world.

Part I reviews Pound's early discovery of Confucianism and his conversion to Confucianism. Pound's interest in Confucianism coincided with the time when Christianity, already "contaminated" by "historical diseases" in Pound's view, could not offer a valid vision to guide the spiritual life, resulting in the loss of self in modern society. Pound discovered three main deficiencies of Christianity — lack of respect for individuality①, the decline of ethics, and an open attack on nature so that it could not provide solutions to Western problems. Pound turned to Confucianism to probe into the existence of modern man in the face of society, and nature, which resulted in Pound's Confucian medicine as a cure for Western moral obtuseness.

Part II focuses on Pound's Confucianism. First, Pound's idea of man and self is explored. It begins with Pound's often-cited ideogram *zhi ren* 知人 (to know men) in *Guide to Kulchur* and develops into Pound's search for making "the real man" "real people" "the complete man" "manhood" "humanity", etc., which are all his translations of *ren* 仁. To know others, to know human nature and to know self are what Pound's *zhi ren* means. Pound's idea of innately good human nature imitated

① Individuality is widely recognized as a social value dominated in Western culture, which highly advocates individual liberty and the distinguished quality of oneself from others. According to Lukes, the individual took shape during the 18th century (Hinchman, 1990: 762). In the English-speaking world, John Stuart Mill, a famous individualist, contributed the most to maintaining the power of the individuality. He wrote in 1840:

> In sober truth...the general tendency of things throughout the world is to render mediocrity the ascendant power among mankind. In ancient history, in the Middle Ages, and in a diminishing degree through the long transition from feudality to the present time, the individual was a power in himself... At present individuals are lost in the crowd. The only power deserving the name is that of masses, and of governments while they make themselves the organ of the tendencies and instincts of masses. This is as true in the moral and social relations of private life as in public transactions... As the various social eminences which enabled persons entrenched on them to disregard the opinion of the multitude gradually become leveled... there ceases to be any social support for nonconformity... (Qtd. in Morgan, 1942: 434)

Morgan (1942: 434) stated: "Since then there have been many protests against forces tending to weaken individuality in the modern world." Ezra Pound, I contend, is one of them because he deplored in 1927: "The drear horror of American life can be traced to two damnable roots, or perhaps it is only one root: The loss of all distinction between public and private affairs." (*SP* 216)

Moreover, during Pound's era, Nicol argued: "The fundamental political problem of today is that of the relations between the individual and the State... But neither is there a way to regulate them while the State and the individual coexist as potentially opposite entities, frequently fighting for their respective spheres of action." For more information, see Eduard Nicol's "Individuality and community" (1949).

Mencius's view, which is *si duan* 四端 ("four beginnings" of human nature). Pound's view of self is complex for it is a combination of Eastern and Western self-orientations — self-criticism and self-enhancement. This self-view has a positive influence on self-development with the ultimate purpose to achieve *ren* 仁. The process of possessing *ren* 仁 is a process of moral development through *xiu shen* 修身 (self-cultivation) in which *cheng* 诚 (sincerity) is pivotal. In short, starting from self to establish personal order is all that a man should consider.

Then it examines Pound's ethics on man and society. According to *Da Xue* (*The Great Learning*, Pound's *The Great Digest*) that Pound had firmly believed in since the mid-1930s, the personal order is the root of the familial order and the social order. Pound held that *xiao ti* 孝悌 (filial piety and fraternal duty) was inevitable and indispensable to establish the familial order. As for building a sound social order, Pound contended that the ruler should take more responsibility than the ordinary people. *Zheng ming* 正名 (the rectification of names), an emblem of Pound's Confucianism, ought to be the first thing the government needs to do, which involves the concept of *li* 礼 (the rites, propriety) embodying the virtue of *yi* 义 (equity and righteousness), which defines the equity of the state. *Wang wang* 王王 (king king), deriving from the Confucian ethics *jun jun chen chen fu fu zi zi* 君君臣臣父父子子, indicates Pound's emphasis on the importance of the head of the state — *yi ren* 一人 in keeping the social order. At the same time, the frequently-recurring term *ben ye* 本业 (namely Pound's *pen yeh*, root occupation) in the later cantos shows that a just social order depends on the power of the masses — everyone completing one's own fundamental occupation.

Then comes Pound's ethics on man and nature①, which analyzes Pound's Confucian metaphysics as a cure for Western philosophical splinters. The harmony between man and nature (*tian ren he yi* 天人合一), the most important philosophical Confucian doctrine, is introduced and illustrated. Beginning with a discussion of

① Nature, as a philosophical term, means different things to different people in different cultures. In this book, the concept of nature is mainly confined in Eastern civilization. In Chinese, the term "nature" may be rendered as either *zi ran* 自然, or *xing* 性, appearing in the early Chinese literature, a "pre-Socratic" sense akin to *Tao* (also *Dao* 道), similar to *fa* 法 (law). Nature, in Confucian metaphysics, has something in common with Confucian *Tian* 天. This book focuses on Pound's concept of nature concerned with Confucianism.

Pound's Confucianism as a totalitarian philosophy①, I explored the nature in Pound's philosophical belief and then probed into *tian ren he yi* from two perspectives — the identity of man's nature and the nature of things, and the union of the way of man and the way of heaven. This part intends to prove that Confucian philosophy can relieve Western society's isolation from nature, remedy the Western moral crises, and lead people to a harmonious existence with nature. Part III sums up Pound's remedy for the West. Pound's Confucian medicine — self-cultivation, social harmony, and the harmonious existence of man and nature heals Western "moral obtuseness" and alienation.

Part III evaluates Pound's Confucianism and the modern world. Pound regarded Confucianism as a remedy for the sick West. The legacy of Pound's Confucianism is discussed in three fields: Poundian scholarship, Confucian scholarship, and amateur readers. This part also explores Pound's Confucianism and modern China. Pound committed himself to transmitting Confucian classics when Confucian temples were destroyed in China, and Confucian beliefs were negated by Western scholars, such as Max Weber and Joseph Levenson. Pound reinstated Confucian values in modern Western society, sharing some inspiring insights into the necessity of realizing modern values of Confucianism in the present world. It is a cause that is being advanced by contemporary New Confucians in response to the challenges of modernity.

---

① Totalitarian philosophy may easily remind readers of the term "totalitarianism". In politics, "totalitarianism, being a dictatorship, characteristically includes the coercive qualities noted in such varied dictatorial systems" (Brzezinski, 1956: 752). In "the intellectual and moral sphere, totalitarianism is the antithesis of ideals of spiritual and mental freedom; it is utterly destructive of the supernatural and absolute bases of our traditional morality; it is, forsooth, a revolt against the continuity of historic civilization" (Hayes, 1938: 23). However, Pound's totalitarian philosophy is quite different from the above-mentioned traditional meaning of totalitarianism. He considered Confucianism as a totalitarian philosophy meaning that Confucianism attaches importance to the whole organic nature, or simply speaking, no splitting from nature.

Part I　Meeting Confucius

"Western contact with the Far East was made in an era of Western degradation. American contact with Japan was forced in the very middle of 'the century of usury.' Western ethics were consummate filth in the middle of the last century." (*SP* 76)

1. Pound and Confucius: A Historical Confrontation

In 1937, Ezra Pound (1885-1972), the self-exiled American poet in Italy, wrote a piece of prose titled "Immediate need of Confucius".

> ...I am writing on the "need for Confucius". I am trying to diagnose Western disease. Western disease has raged for over two centuries. Western disease shows in sixty percent racket on ink money. That is a *symptom* of moral obtuseness. (*SP* 76)

Pound briefly explained the "need for Confucius" in the same work: "A 'need' implies a lack, a sick man has 'need.' Something he has not." (*SP* 79) In Pound's view, the West was sick and suffered from "moral obtuseness". Pound subsequently put forward a tentative proposal to heal the disease afflicting the West: "Kung as medicine?" (*SP* 79) Ending his three-word-sentence with a question mark indicated Pound's uncertainty of his prescription. Pound, however, bent himself to seeking the best medicine for the sick West.

One year later, in *Guide to Kulchur* (1938), Pound began the book with "DIGEST OF THE ANALECTS", and later in the same book, he wrote an essay "KUNG" (Confucius) in which he spoke highly of Confucius ideas on life, agriculture and economics. He maintained that the charm of Confucianism was not to "petrify thought" (*GK* 277) but to "MAKE IT NEW" (*GK* 278).

> His (Confucius's) thought is never something scaled off the surface of facts. It is root volition branching out, the ethical weight is present in every phrase. (*GK* 279)

With Pound's deep involvement in Confucianism, he became more and more certain of his Confucian prescription, which was well manifested in his poetry, prose, translations, letters and etc. Pound's commitment to his self-appointed mission — to remedy the West with Confucianism — concentrated on his ideological engagement throughout his career as a poet, critic and translator.

As a modern poet, Pound was sensitive to contemporary social issues. He diagnosed the contemporary Western society as morally declining and dedicated his life to the cure of the decline. After almost two decades of diagnosing and contemplating, Pound prescribed Confucianism for the sick West. However, some questions may be asked: Was the West really ill? And was the medicine suited for the illness? To answer these questions, we need to look back to the European past and look into the situations during the age when Pound lived.

Tracing back to the years when Pound fervently advocated Confucianism, the study finds out two historical environments inspiring Pound to promote the significance of Confucianism: One is the perplexing ideological environment and the other is the unfavorable intellectual environment.

1.1 The Perplexing Ideological Environment

The 18th century when the Industrial Revolution started, according to Pound, was probably the onset of the sickness of the West. In the middle of the 18th century, the Industrial Revolution started in the midland of England and rapidly spread to the whole area of Europe. In the 19th century, it reached North America. With the coming of the 19th century, however, the British Empire, the empire on which "the sun had never set", began to decline. Although Great Britain was the cradle of the Industrial Revolution, she couldn't always lead the way. Towards the end of the 19th century, some newly-industrialized countries, which developed more quickly than Britain, became Britain's rivals not only for new sources of raw materials but also for new markets for manufactured goods. In 1900, Britain was surpassed by the United States and Germany in industrial production, and Britain lost its supremacy in the world's economy (Barber, 2006: 313).

The 19th century witnessed the scientific and technological advancement on the one hand and growing pains and wars in Europe on the other hand. All of these triggered intriguing new ideologies, and one of the most influential ones in Europe in the late 19th and early 20th centuries was Marxism. In 1848, the German philosophers Karl Marx and Friedrich Engels published their seminal work *The Communist Manifesto*, in which Marx and Engels combined 18th-century French Enlightenment, German post-Kantian philosophy, English classical political economy and early 19th-century European utopian socialism. Marxism came to be very influential. For example, Marxist humanism, which was called the Alienation (Entfremdung) Theory, changed European views of Christianity. The Marxist theory maintains that the social alienation or the estrangement of people from aspects of their human nature is based on *The Essence of Christianity* (1841) by Ludwig Feuerbach, which argues that the supernatural idea of "God" has alienated the natural characteristics of the human beings. In his early writing, *The Economic and Philosophic Manuscripts of 1844* (1927), Marx expressed his Alienation Theory and categorized alienation as having four types: 1) alienation of a worker from the work — from the product of his labour; 2) alienation of a worker from working — from the act of producing; 3) alienation of a worker from himself, as a producer — from his Gattungswesen (species-essence); 4) alienation of a worker from other workers.

Europe at this time was Christian. Pound clearly knew the dominant role of religions, especially Christianity, in the lives of Europeans. He once remarked in a heavily jesting tone: "Because there are people who acknowledge that the Church is bankrupt it is ridiculous to assume that Europe is naturally without religion." (*MAW* 134) Deeply rooted in Europe, after the Christian reformation in the 16th and 17th centuries, Christianity had actually united the European countries after the 1700s. However, it was confronted with challenges from different fields starting around the 19th century. Apart from the above Marxist alienation, which shocked pious Christians, another challenge was undoubtedly C. R. Darwin's *On the Origin of Species* published in 1859. It immediately rocked the Christian world. Darwin's theory of evolution encountered strong and immediate opposition from Christian theologians. They abruptly revolted against Darwin's theory, which substituted an automatic natural mechanism for the Creator's designed creation. Theological opposition to Darwin's theory was publicized at a meeting of the British Association for the Advancement of Science at Oxford in 1860 when the Bishop of Oxford attacked the leading exponent of Darwinism, namely the biologist Thomas Huxley. An unexpected influence of Darwinism was on social science. Although Darwin did not attempt to apply the principle of natural selection to sociology by himself, Herbert Spencer (1820-1903), an English philosopher and sociologist who was greatly impressed by Darwin, applied Darwin's theory to the development of the human society. Spencer substituted the "survival of the fittest" for the term "natural selection". Spencer's term became a slogan for those who sought to apply Darwin's evolutionary principles to society, which resulted in the so-called social Darwinism. This theory advocated cutthroat competition and the *laissez faire* policy as the keys to the struggle for social existence.

Philosophically, Christianity faced another serious challenge from the German philosopher Friedrich Nietzsche, one of the darkest 19th-century philosophers. He believed "that religion, particularly Christianity…always repressed the individual and discouraged creativity" (Barber, 2006: 340). One of his best-known iconic remarks was "God is dead". This statement expressed his strong desire to free the individuals' will. He argued that the "individual as manifested in the superman should be the goal of man" and "man should not be satisfied with being part of the herd"①. Historians commented that the Nietzschean thought that was "combined with aggressive German nationalism" "contributed to the rise of a new Germany in the interwar years under Hitler" (Barber, 2006: 340). The death of God led to outright Nihilism, a belief that nothing had any inherent importance and life lacked any purpose. Nietzsche stated that Christianity could be an antidote against the primal form of Nihilism because the Christian moral doctrines offered humans an intrinsic value — belief in God. Therefore, Nietzschean philosophy consequently put the man in a dilemma: On the one hand, it freed man's will from Jesus' oppression; on the other hand, it drove the man to "the desert of belief" — belief in nothing or "will to nothingness" in the Nietzschean term.

Nietzsche finally went mad with the coming of the turmoil of the 20th century. Kenneth Auchincloss defined the 20th century as "the age of soldiers smoking in foxholes and women entering the labor force; an era in which ordinary folks changed history"②. He sketched a panorama of Europe with such a concise sentence. The theme of the first half of the 20th century was the competition of state power which ended with world wars. During World War I, battles spread across Europe. The battles turned the world upside down and exhausted Europe. One profound and lasting effect of the war was that "the collective psyche of Europe was almost irreparably damaged" (Barber, 2006: 339). The terrible trauma lingered on for nearly a century. The destruction and chaos of the wars made many people not believe what they had known and believed before. What made it worse was that people with anxiety could not draw comfort from God. French existentialists, such as Jean-Paul Sartre, denied the existence of God, and said that man just appeared. Man as a free individual defined his own existence, and man had no choice but to act, to act on his own.

The war left Europe in a state of shock, confusion and anxiety, which was depicted in the art, music and literature of the time. The turn-of-the-century science

① The information is from the following website: http://en.wikipedia.org/wiki/Friedrich_Nietzsche#Death_of_God_and_nihilism [2018-05-10].

② Kenneth Auchincloss was a long-time *Newsweek* editor who wrote an essay in the last edition of *Newsweek* published in December 1999. In this article named "Fanfare for the common man", he claimed that the 20th century was "an era in which ordinary folks changed history". At the end of the essay, he reiterated that "the common man has more control over his life — new choices, but also new dilemmas".

also made Europeans unsure of the world and the future. As Auchincloss (1999) argued: "Old assumptions have been challenged right and left, but it has been difficult to replace them with any new certainties — in fact, the very notion of certainty is alien to the 20th-century cast of mind." He subsequently threw out his opinion: "Blame the physicists." In 1905, Albert Einstein published his Theory of Relativity in which he argued that space and time were not absolute but relative, with the only constant through both space and time being the speed of light. In 1927, Werner Heisenberg put forward his confusing Uncertainty Principle in which he stated that in subatomic experiments neither the position nor the velocity of a particle could be determined at the same time. It had astonishing consequences: Reality was distorted and humans became agents determining what's there. Such scientific discoveries left Europeans in a world of uncertainty, unsettlement and absence of absolute truth. As stated above, it was also in the year 1927 that Marx's early writing *The Economic and Philosophic Manuscripts of 1844* that contained his Alienation Theory was published. Europeans were consequently alienated, estranged and separated from God, society and their own self, witnessing the horrible destruction of the war, and confronting with unsettled philosophies and confusing scientific theories. And then World War II made everything worse.

Ezra Pound lived in such an unordered and lost Europe. As an outstanding pioneer of post-war poetry, he had a penetrating insight into modern Europe. In "European Paideuma"① (1940), he stated: "It is some four hundred years since the Church started on its path of moral and spiritual bankruptcy. For this usury and the revival of ancient Jewish texts (*Old Testament*) may, in part, have been responsible." (*MAW* 133) Early in 1937, he claimed: "The Church had lost its faith anyhow, and mess, unholy and slithering mess, supervened." "The Church of England…remained a bulwark of usury." (*SP* 77) Pound ascribed Europe's illness to religion and usury. He remarked: "Its (the Church) decline began with a flight from reality." (*MAW* 133) Furthermore, Pound poignantly pointed to another problem of Western civilization: "Greek philosophy was almost an attack upon nature", or in other words, "philosophy splinter…splint away from organic nature" (*SP* 87).

Pound never ceased to ponder a serious question — how to save the West? Instead of appealing to order from Greco-Roman mythology like T. S. Eliot and James

① Pound published the essay "European Paideuma" in 1940 which was collected in *Machine Art and Other Writings: The Lost Thought of the Italian Years* (Ed. by M. L. Ardizzone. Durham: Duke University Press. 1996).

Joyce, Pound delved into Eastern culture — Confucianism[①] and chose a historic figure rather than a mythological one to save "the Waste Land" in Eliot's words. A tentative reassurance in Confucianism and a brave reformation of Western economics and politics were pervasive in his poetry, essays, letters, broadcasts and Confucian translations. For instance, Stead (1986: 278) argued that Cantos LII-LXXI, also named as the "China Cantos" and Adam's cantos, were "obsessively concerned with the Just Society" and "also the man bent on changing the world". Pound's endeavor to transmit Confucianism from the East to the West so as to remedy the West was similar to some main principles of the third generation of the 20th-century New Confucianism.[②] Little did Pound know that his ideas would be so prophetic.

1.2 The Unfavorable Intellectual Environment

Pound enthusiastically embraced Confucianism, though Confucianism was under an unprecedented attack in China and was at a low ebb in the West. Pound knew about what Confucianism was confronted with in China. In 1914, he helped a Chinese official, Faxiang Song (Far-son T. Sung 宋发祥), publish an essay "The poverty of China" in which Song attacked Confucius's indifference to materialistic enjoyment and ascribed China's poverty to the sage. Although Pound managed to publish this article so as to make a proper response to his Chinese friend's commission, it didn't necessarily mean that Pound shared the same idea with Song. Pound's disapproval was evident in his introductory note to the essay: "I might excerpt the passage whereof I disapprove." (Qian, 2006: 163) In the West, Confucianism was no longer in favor. Enlightenment thinkers such as Max Weber declared it as a backward value system. The tradition of Confucianism was widely deemed dying and in the hopeless decline.

① Confucianism (*ruxue* 儒学), simply speaking, is ethical and philosophical thoughts developed from Confucius's (孔子) sayings. According to Weiming Tu, the representative figure of New Confucianism, Confucianism saw three epochs: the classical pre-Han Confucianism, Song-Ming Neo-Confucianism and New Confucianism. For detailed information, visit the website http://en.wikipedia.org/wiki/New_Confucianism [2018-05-20].

② New Confucianism is an intellectual movement of Confucianism that began at the beginning of the 20th century in China and further developed since the 1980s. It advocates the reinterpretation of Confucian ideas to deal with modern problems in a contemporary context, and promotes social, ecological and political harmony in synthesis with Western philosophies such as rationalism and humanism. New Confucian scholars emerged from Chinese and developed to non-Asians, and its forum also extended from China (including Taiwan and Hong Kong) to the United States of America. At present, New Confucianism is widely recognized in the third generation represented by Weiming Tu and Zhongying Cheng with efforts to solve problems generated in the modern society through Confucianism. For detailed information, consult Makeham, J. 2003. *New Confucianism: A Critical Examination*. Hampshire: Palgrave Macmillan.

William Loftus Hare's "Chinese egoism" on the *Egoist* on December 1st, 1914, was one piece of evidence of the decline of Confucianism in the West. In "Chinese egoism", Hare valued Yang Zhu's hedonist assumption — "a person's joy is in the world's rich materials", but he belittled Confucius "with an everlasting reputation, who never had a day's gaiety". Pound published his article "The words of Ming Mao 'Least among the disciples of Kung-Fu-Tse'" as a rejoinder to Hare and Song (Qian, 2006: 164). Pound's response to Western orientalists and Chinese modernists proved that he knew that Confucianism was withering away in both the Orient and the Occident. Probably that's the reason why Pound appointed himself a mission, as he declared at the end of Canto XIII, to keep the Confucian "apricot blossoms" from falling.

2. Pound's Conversion to Confucianism*

"One of Ezra Pound's most stimulating books"①, *Guide to Kulchur*, begins with "DIGEST OF THE ANALECTS". On the first page of that short chapter, four Chinese characters, followed by their English translations, are inserted. They occupy the middle position of the page.

I have reduced it all to one principle.

一
以
贯
之 (*GK* 15)

"One principle" Pound learned and insisted on should be Confucianism. Later in the same book, the four characters in the center are justified again in Chapter 17 "Sophists" (*GK* 125). Actually, Pound didn't just adhere to "one principle". But it doesn't mean that he has shifted from Confucianism. In his late years, Pound, without knowing it himself, encompassed other philosophic ideas such as Buddhism and Taoism (which are not the focuses in this book).

Pound's conversion to a Confucian believer was not a sudden decision; his spiritual quest permeated his controversial life. It was T. S. Eliot who first questioned Pound's belief. Eliot's famous inquiry "what does Mr. Pound believe" became a highly-quoted question when Pound's belief was under discussion. Pound's first direct response to Eliot took place two years later in *Credo* (1930): "I have for a number of years answered such questions by telling the enquirer to read Confucius and Ovid." (*SP* 53) Four years later, in 1934, Pound became more certain and made an announcement rather than an answer to Eliot's question in an article "Date line":

---

* Parts of this chapter have been published as an essay titled "Pound's conversion to Confucianism" in *Journal of Literature and Art Studies*, 2014, (3): 165-173. Thank the journal for allowing me to collect the essay in this book. There're some changes from the original essay.

① See the back cover of Pound's book *Guide to Kulchur*.

As to what I believe:
I believe the *Ta Hio* (*LE* 86)

In his first answer to Eliot's question, he avoided the terminology "believe" but provided an alternative to his "enquirer", but in 1934 he vowed his singular faith "I believe the *Ta Hio* (*The Great Learning*)". That is the *Da Xue*, one of the "Four Books". In 1955, Pound reiterated his belief by referring to its Japanese title, in Canto LXXXVIII "I believe the Dai Gaku" (601)[①].

Pound showed his worries about the West in his prose "Immediate need of Confucius". He maintained:

> The life of Occidental mind fell apart into progressively stupider and still more stupid segregations. The Church of England for example remained a bulwark or usury and/or a concatenation of sinecures, for the holding whereof neither courage, character nor intelligence was required or even wanted. (*SP* 77)

Pound's ardent involvement in Confucianism kept abreast of his worry about "the life of Occidental mind" and his disbelief in Christianity.

2.1 Pound's Denunciation of Christianity

The three stages of Pound's dealing with Confucianism clearly show his conversion to Confucianism. His conversion actually originated from his contemplation on the disordered Western society. In his view, "today the whole Occident is bathed daily in mental sewage" (*SP* 76). He pursued what Confucianism could offer and what the West lacked. His fondness for Confucianism kept abreast of his aversion to religion, especially Christianity. "A religion is damned, it confesses its own ultimate impotence, the day it burns its first heretic." (*SP* 52) As for Pound, Christianity degenerated and "the Church had lost its faith anyhow, and mess, unholy and slithering mess, supervened" (*SP* 77). "Fall of Church" already pushed Europeans into a "time when Church no longer had faith ENOUGH to believe that with proper instruction and argument the unbeliever or heretic could be made to see daylight" (*SP*

① All quotations from *The Cantos* are taken from the ninth paperbound printing (first published paperbound as NDP 824 in 1996). Information on quotations is given in parentheses where the Roman number, if necessary, is the number of the canto and the Arabic number the page number.

61). As a matter of fact, Pound asserted: "Christianity and/or religion in the anglo-saxon world of our time has been something optional. Some of us went to church in our childhood and some didn't." (*GK* 26) As a result, "'belief' as the pious once used the term is alien to our age" (*GK* 26). Just as stated in Chapter 1, modern Europeans had lost faith in Christianity. Pound's unfavorable comment on Christianity went with his favorable intention toward Confucianism. Contrasting Confucianism with Christianity, he found three main problems of Christianity: Firstly, Christianity had degenerated into deprivation of individual liberty; secondly, it flees from reality and fails to provide the ethics that teaches man a way of living; thirdly, its emphasis on human power results in a violent conquest of nature.

The first and foremost problem of Christianity, as Pound revealed in his "Imaginary letters VII" (1918), went as follows:

> Christianity...has reduced itself to one principle: "Thou shalt attend to thy neighbour's business in preference to thine own." It is upon this basis that the churches are organized, it is upon this basis that they flourish, (bar one old established conspirator's club which exploits a more complicated scenic arrangement). (*PD* 71)

The essential nature of Christianity, in Pound's view, was to spy into others' lives rather than focus on one's own. Later, in 1921, Pound's condemnation against religion became pungent and merciless — the organized religions were usually "exploitation, control of the masses" and the greatest tyranny derived from Christian dogma that imposed its will upon the individual (*SP* 50). Religious belief, in Pound's definition, was "a cramp, and thence progressively a paralysis or atrophy of the mind" (*SP* 52) and here the Nietzschean tendency in Pound was found. But Pound didn't deny the existence of God. At the beginning of the same essay "Axiomata", Pound announced: "God...exists" and "the universe exists" (*SP* 49). Nevertheless, Pound's God was not the religious God but an ethical God who could guide and teach people to live in the earthly world. Religion, according to Pound's essay on Arnold Dolmetsch, began with myth. The decline of the cult began when the core of subjective experience congealed into dogma, and the cultists attempted to impose it on others (Jackson, 1968: 74).

Confucius's pursuit of individual freedom intrigued his interest and also permeated his first stage of Confucianism. The long stanza (lines 5-30) of Canto XIII contributes to Pound's special finding — respect for individuality. The section portraying the conversation between Confucius and his four disciples comes from *Lun Yu* XI. 25, in which Confucius asked his disciples what they would do if one day they "become known", and in which Confucius encouraged his disciples to express themselves freely. Their answers are almost the same as that of Pauthier's and Legge's translations on which Pound's rendering depended heavily, and also the same as that of Pound's own version in "Imaginary letters VII" and his translation of *Lun Yu* about 20 years later. The most striking difference between the version of this poem and those of various translations is that Pound's poetic Confucius responded differently after the last disciple uttered his answer. In Pound's translation as well as in the narration of "Imaginary letters VII", Pound created a Confucius in accordance with the one in the original text by responding agreeably "I am rather of Si-hoa's opinion" (*PD* 73) and "I am with Chieh" (*Con* 243). But in the poem, "Kung smiled upon all of them equally". Confucius made no distinction between Dian's (曾点, Pound's Si-hoa or Chieh) answer and the other three's. Moreover, his comment made his intention clearer: "They have all answered correctly, / That is to say, each in his nature." (Canto XIII 58) Here, the poet invented a Confucius who evaluated his disciple each "in his nature" and was "equally" pleased with their ideas. Such adaption aimed at liberalizing Confucius and meeting his emphasis on individual liberty.

In Confucian scholarship, the above-mentioned section of *Lun Yu*, as Lan (2005: 96) stated, had not been given such close attention as Pound gave it. In a traditional fashion, this section was usually read as exemplifying Confucius's expectation of modesty as the character of a proper statesman. But Pound found the significance of this section in the Confucian notion of free speech, which was associated with his beloved Dantesque notion of free will: "Who forbids you to express it? Here each one may say what he likes." (*PD* 72) During the years when Pound wrote Canto XIII, he concentrated on exploring the automatic self and egoism. Actually, he made every effort to establish his own identity in his early poems, such as *Personae* (1909). Several years later, he recalled this self-exploring experience in an essay on "Vorticism":

> In the "search for oneself," in the search for "sincere self-expression," one gropes, one finds some seeming verity. One says, "I'm this, that, or the other, and with the words scarcely uttered one ceases to be that thing. I began this search for the real in a book called *Personae*, casting off, as it were, complete masks of the self in each poem." (*GB* 85)

Of course, the foregoing statements are usually considered with Pound's search for his distinguished voice in poetry; they are not merely technical exercises, as Witemeyer (1969: 85) argued, but a part of the search for the real, for himself, for "sincere self-expression".

The second problem of Christianity is "a flight from reality" (*MAW* 133) and it's "little concern[ed] with ethics" (*SR* 95). In Canto XIII, the useless metaphysical-theological speculation was condemned by Kung's saying "nothing of the 'life after death'" (Canto XIII 59). The decline of Christianity, in Pound's view, "began with a flight from reality" (*MAW* 133). Pound once claimed: "The essence of religion is the present tense." (*SP* 70)

"The *present* tense" was used to highlight the importance of practice or action in real life. Pound made a further movement to condemn European civilization: "If you squint at European thought from one angle it will appear to burrow into the schools and say farewell to reality." (*GK* 30) The well-known announcement about Pound's belief is that "I believe the *Ta Hio*". The *Ta Hio* was published in 1928, heavily based on Pauthier's French version of the "Four Books". There's little doubt that *The Great Learning* initially intrigued Pound and profoundly influenced him. What intrigued Pound seems to be the practical nature of *The Great Learning*. Nolde (1983: 19) argued: "There was nothing mystical or metaphysical about it. Here was a practical, ethical system divorced from any religion or religious institution." He continued: "It pointed a way to world peace and harmony which did not require priests and churches and dogma." For Pound, Christianity failed to provide people a way of life. In fact, early in 1910, Pound realized "Christianity and all other forms of ecstatic religion...*seem* little concerned with ethics" (*SR* 95). Later in his essay "Ecclesiastical history" (1934), he ascribed "the decline of Christian ethics" to "economic corruption" (*SP* 61). However, Pound had a penetrating insight into Confucian ethics. In "On the degrees of honesty in various Occidental religions", Pound claimed that "it appears to me that Confucius has in his dimension a pre-eminence over other founders of ethical systems; while yielding nothing to any of them in other domains" (*SP* 68). In the same prose, he analyzed one reason why Christianity couldn't reside in the mind of Chinese:

> It is quite certain that Christianity appears or has in known instances appeared both immoral and anti-statal to the serious Chinese literate. He saw it as such when the Jesuits were inserting it into China in the seventeenth and eighteenth centuries. Disruptive of family life, disturbing to the quiet and order of the empire, inducing disrespect to the dead and destructive to Confucian ethics. (*SP* 65)

To put it shortly, Christianity is "destructive to Confucian ethics". A year later in 1940, his condemnation of Christianity became more obvious: "It may be said here that the followers of Confucius and of Mencius were horrified at the immoral and anti-social nature of Christianity and for a long time kept it out of China on those grounds." (*MAW* 133)

Another problem of Christianity, which it shares with Greek philosophy, lies in the fact that it's "almost an attack upon nature" (*SP* 86), but "at no point does the Confucio-Mencian ethic or philosophy splinter and split away from organic nature" (*SP* 87). Nature, in Pound's world, has a profound meaning, which will be discussed in detail in Part II. As he highly praised nature, he strongly denounced anything which was contra nature. In his poetry and prose, he ceaselessly condemned usury being "CONTRA NATURAM" (Canto XLV 230):

> …the usurer is damned with the sodomite. Usury judged with sodomy as "contrary to natural increase", contrary to the nature of live things (animal and vegetable) to multiply. (*SP* 61)

As for Pound, "this usury and revival of ancient Jewish texts (*Old Testament*) may, in part, have been responsible" for the "moral and spiritual bankruptcy" of the Church (*MAW* 133). Unlike Christ, who "founded an ethics of the soul and its afterlife" (Cheadle, 1997: 18), "Confucius offers a way of life, an Anschauung or disposition toward nature and man and a system for dealing with both" (*GK* 24). Liang (梁漱溟, 2017: 213) also maintained that the way of Confucius was a way of life rather than of thought.

Another reason for Pound's strong opposition to Christianity was that Christianity is monotheistic. In Pound's view, "the glory of the polytheistic anschauung is that it never asserted a single and obligatory path for everyone. It never caused the assertion that everyone was fit for initiation and it never caused an attempt to force people into a path alien to their sensibilities" (*SP* 56). Pound hated despotism and valued the right of differences to exist. In "Religio", Pound asked and answered:

> What is a god?
> A god is an eternal state of mind.
> …
> What is the greatest hearsay?
> The greatest hearsay is the tradition of the gods. (*SP* 47)

"The tradition of the gods", the author believes, refers to the mythology spoken highly of by Pound.

Comparing the Catholic Church with Protestantism, Pound preferred the former. He referred to Martin Luther as "merely a barbarian bore" and declared "Protestantism has no theology" at all (*SP* 57). In the detention camp at Pisa, when Pound was allowed to speak to one person each day, "he picked the camp's Catholic chaplain" (Flory, 2003: 147). The chaplain Pound chose was Father Aloysius Vath. He wondered "why Pound, who was not a Catholic, had chosen a priest rather than one of the two Protestant ministers". Pound answered: "What can the other guys tell me? You can tell me something." The chaplain recalled: "He asked me a lot about the Catholic religion." On 26 June 1945, Father Aloysius Vath claimed: "For a Confucianist and a Catholic, we get along very well." (Flory, 2003: 147) Pound's preference for Catholicism rather than Protestantism probably results from "Directions for Confession". "Pound is developing his larger point, about the compatibility of Confucianism and Catholicism, by noting the importance of the disciplines of self-examination in both." (Flory, 2003: 147)

Having totally lost faith in Christianity, Pound finally turned to Confucianism. He wrote in his 1939 prose "Degrees of honesty in Occidental religions":

> I might almost say that for a period of nearly fifty years I have never met Christian FAITH ... Confucian faith I can conceive. I can conceive of a man's believing that if, and in measure as, he brings order into his own consciousness (his own "innermost") that order will emanate from him. The cycle of Chinese history, the reception of the "mandate" (called the mandate of heaven) by various dynasties, seems to offer demonstrable evidence of this process. (*SP* 66)

Obviously, Pound recognized that the core of Confucianism was a harmony created by the unity of the inner transcendence and the mandate of heaven. He ended this prose by comparing Confucianism and Christianity:

> Both Confucianism and Christianity propose a state of sincerity which is almost unattainable, but the Christian proposals are mixed with all sorts of disorder, whereas a Confucian progress offers chance for a steady rise, and defects either in conduct or in theory are in plain violation of its simple and central doctrine. (*SP* 69)

The ending delivers two profound meanings. On the one hand, the purpose of pursuing a kind of spiritual state, "which is almost unattainable", makes Confucianism and Christianity similar. In Confucianism, the almost-unreachable state is called *zhong yong* 中庸 (Pound's pivot); in Christianity, it may be a kind of state in which ordinary people can talk with God through prayer. On the other hand, Pound attached great importance to the spiritual elevation of an individual. He found that Confucian believers got chances to improve themselves steadily and constantly — that's a process of establishing the order within the self. But Christian believers suffered from "all sorts of disorder" and chaos on the way to achieving that holy state, so he declared: "I see almost no spiritual elevation in the *Old Testament*, and the *Talmud.*" (*SP* 68)

2.2 Becoming a Confucian Poet

Pound's Confucianism has been grouped into three phases by Poundian scholars. Lan (2005: 3) categorized Pound's Confucianism into three periods: 1) imitative — from early years of contacting Confucianism to the year of 1928; 2) creative — from the early 1930s to the end of World War II; 3) comprehensive — after World War II. Cheadle (1997: 9) offered a similar classification: Pound's Confucianism began in about 1910, and developed into the certainty of "belief" only after about two decades (about 1930); the second period ran from the 1930s to the first half of the 1940s; the last period was after World War II and the fall of Mussolini's Italy. Moreover, there are no remarkably divergent views on Pound's Confucianism in the first two periods. Namely, the first period is marked with Pound's strong interest in individual freedom and social responsibility; the second period is characterized by his fervent enthusiasm for the social order accompanying his polemic political views; as for the third period, however, the opinions of the two main Poundian scholars are a little different. Cheadle (1997: 9) considered "this last phase of his Confucianism is marked by a return to what he (Pound) regarded as Confucian fundamentals, with a concern for precise verbal definitions at the center of them all". Nevertheless, Lan (2005: 5) argued: "Pound's postwar cantos were characterized by an arduous spiritual quest sustained by, among other things, his extensive quotations from Confucian texts and his intensified inscription of a Confucian anthropocosmic vision." Between the two views, the author has a more favorable attitude towards Lan's than Cheadle's, i.e. Pound served as a real liberal Confucian disciple who pursued inner growth of mind in the last period of his Confucianism.

What the author wants to express is that Pound developed a comparatively comprehensive understanding of Confucianism in his "imitative" phase. To put it in another way, he established Confucian ethics in the first phase of his involvement with

Confucianism. So what he insisted upon and extended during his second and third periods could not be diverted from his fundamental recognition of Confucianism in the first period. His comparatively comprehensive understanding of Confucianism is well manifested in his first Confucian canto — Canto XIII, which will be discussed shortly. It may be said that his lifelong devotion to Confucianism started with his disappointment and doubt of Christianity in his early academic years because, as a member of the mainstream Western culture, Christianity could not provide a way to cope with a serious Western problem — alienation. Pound's Confucianism, as Cheadle (1997: 9) argued, is "born from his discontent with traditional Western monotheism". Monotheism, simply speaking, is Christianity. Pound's repudiation of Christianity never ceased during his life, and his belief in Confucianism was never static.

The first period of Pound's Confucianism can be divided into two phases: a random study and a serious study. In the phase of random study, Pound benefited from several scholars among whom some are prominent Orientalists who led him to know Confucius as well as Chinese poetry. In the phase of serious study, outstanding achievement is the publication of Canto XIII. This phase culminated in 1928 with his first English translation of *Da Xue*, which was rendered from Pauthier's French version of the "Four Books".

Pound's early contact with Confucianism started with his parents' interest in a Christian mission in China. According to Noel Stock (2011: 176), Pound probably read some Confucius "as early as July, 1907". Laurence Binyon (1869-1943), an English poet and Oriental art historian in the British Museum, opened a door for Pound to step through and into the real palace of Oriental paintings. Pound became a frequent visitor to Binyon, who at that time served as the assistant keeper of the British Museum in charge of the collection of Far Eastern paintings and color prints, and who vigorously worked on expatiating upon the nature and monuments of Chinese art. Pound regularly "ate at the WIENER CAFÉ" (Canto LXXX 526) near the British Museum with Binyon's group, and their conversation definitely expanded his interest in some specific topics associated with Oriental art. Pound cherished the good memories of his time with Binyon, and about three decades later, he recalled his early days in London in his *Pisan Cantos* as "the British Museum era" (Canto LXXX 526). He mourned "the loss of that cafe (in 1914) / meant the end of a B. M. era" when "the WIENER CAFÉ" "died into banking". Pound also expressed his heartfelt gratitude to Binyon several lines later: "So it is to Mr. Binyon that I owe, initially." (Canto LXXX 527) In Canto LXXXVII (592), when he had been deeply, and almost totally, involved in Confucianism, he highly praised Binyon by comparing him to sequoias with the lines as follows: "Only sequoias are slow enough. / BinBin 'is beauty'. / 'Slowness is beauty.'" All these — his attendance at Binyon's lectures, those conversations in Binyon's group and his frequent visits to the British Museum to inspect the collection of Chinese and Japanese paintings — offered Pound a preliminary education in Oriental art and aroused his lifelong attachment to the Chinese traditional culture.

The real mentor, however, who led Pound to Chinese literature and Chinese classics, was Allen Upward (1863-1926), the author of the Confucian anthology, *The Sayings of K'ung the Master* (1904). Two of Upward's books influenced Pound: One was *The New Word* (published in 1907 but originally written in 1901), and the other was *Scented Leaves — from a Chinese Jar*. The former caught Pound's attention regarding the ideas of Kung, while the latter was the one that triggered Pound's real curiosity about Chinese poetry and stimulated Pound to go "down to Upward's family home in the Isle of Wight to soak some of it up" at the end of September 1913 (Carpenter, 1988: 218). Upward had no knowledge of the Chinese language, and he explained to Pound that the sequence of poems in the *Scented Leaves — from a Chinese Jar* was made up out of his mind with the help of "a certain amount of Chinese reminiscence" (Carpenter, 1988: 218). Upward showed Pound the book from which he got the inspiration — H. A. Giles's *A History of Chinese Literature* (1901) and also encouraged Pound to read Pauthier's *Les Quatres Lives de Philosophie Morale et Politique de la Chine* (1841). Pound not only admired Upward's "esoteric knowledge of folklore and anthropology" (Carpenter, 1988: 218), but also highly appreciated Upward's thought. In 1945 Pound compared Upward's mind with those of Plato and Bacon in *The Pisan Canto*: "'the mind of Plato...or that of Bacon' said Upward / seeking parallel for his own." (Canto LXXVII 489) The master Kung was highly praised by Upward for his wisdom and his refusal to talk about the unknown in *The New Word* (索金梅, 2003: 18). About ten years later, after he met Upward, Pound claimed: "Kung said nothing of the 'life after death.'" (Canto XIII 59)

Pound did not begin a rigorous study of the Confucian classics in 1913, Cheadle (1997: 11) argued. But it didn't mean that his "looking at" Pauthier's works left nothing on his mind because he wrote to Dorothy on 2 October 1913: "I'm stocked up with K'ung fu Tsze, and Men Tsze, etc. I suppose they'll keep me calm for a week or so." (Carpenter, 1988: 219) Pound gained strength and calmness from his "looking at" Chinese classics, which directed his potential devotion to Confucianism. He was attracted by "Chinese colour". Under the inspiration of Upward's *Scented Leaves —*

from a Chinese Jar, he wrote a poem "A Song of the Degrees", which was published in the *Poetry* in November 1913: "Rest me with Chinese colours / For I think the glass is evil." (Qian, 1995:186)

Mary Fenollosa, the widow of Ernest Fenollosa (1853-1908), appeared just at the right time when Pound was eager to compose poems with "Chinese colour". Pound himself said in "Date line": "Fenollosa's work was given me in a manuscript when I was ready for it. It saved me a great deal of time." (*LE* 77) Ernest Fenollosa was an enthusiastic Orientalist, and his sudden death in 1908 left much work undone. One of his unfinished works was Chinese and Japanese materials contained in his notebook. Pound met Mrs. Fenollosa in the fall of 1913. Their meeting accelerated Pound's conversion to Confucianism, and stimulated his enthusiasm for Chinese and Japanese poetry. Ernest Fenollosa was the scholar who influenced Pound most and finally assisted him in becoming a "Confucian poet" (Palandri, 1974: 301). Fenollosa's notebook started Pound's fervent study of Chinese poetry, which resulted in the distinguished work *Cathay* (1915) that earned him the fame as "the inventor of Chinese poetry for our time"① and other works such as *Certain Noble Plays of Japan* (1916) and *The Chinese Written Character as a Medium for Poetry* (1919).

Pound started his serious study of Confucianism in around 1915, resulting in the publication of Canto XIII (1925). Canto XIII was composed in 1923 and published in 1925 with *A Draft of XVI Cantos*. The Confucian ethics Pound established in the short canto provided a panorama of Confucianism for the whole epic. During the years composing Canto XIII, he concentrated on individuality, but he also presented the Confucian order and the unity of man and nature in the poems. The two major themes have been already explored and widely accepted by Poundian scholars, such as Lan's (2005: 106) "respect for the 'nature' of the individual and an appeal to social order" and Cheadle's (1997: 22) "individual integrity and social cohesion". Their foci, however, are somewhat different. Lan concentrated on interpreting and demonstrating "a tension" created by the two themes and "its charm" sustained in them. Cheadle discussed the two topics respectively, but failed to find the dynamic interaction between them.

What the author stresses is that respect for individuality②, as regards to Pound, is his search for his distinguished voice in poetry as well as a part of his search for the

---

① T. S. Eliot called Ezra Pound "the inventor of Chinese poetry for our time" in the introduction to *Selected Poems of Ezra Pound* (Pound, 1973: 14).

② "Confucian respect for individuality" means respect for the nature of the individuals.

real self. As for the second widely-accepted theme, "an appeal to social order" is Pound's intention to identify a human being's position in the society. In his 1938 prose "Mang Tse", Pound showed special preference to the words written "on the bo leaves" so as to call for that "we in the West *need* to begin the first chapter of the *Ta Hio*, not merely to grant a casual admission of it in some out-house of our ethics or of our speculations" (*SP* 77). Another theme I've discovered is Pound's concern for nature. Canto XIII begins with Confucius' peaceful walk "by the dynastic temple" "into the cedar grove", and "then out by the lower river" (Canto XIII 58). Such poetic lines of landscape description create a tranquil picture of an environment-friendly life, and convey a hint of beauty and serenity beyond our imagination. The harmonious atmosphere implies the ideal existence of man and nature. The pursuit of the unity of himself with nature originates from the early years of his career, and extends deeply and broadly into his later cantos.

In short, the Confucian ethics built in Canto XIII deals with "respect for individuality", the establishment of the social order, and a concern for nature. Conclusively speaking, Canto XIII is Pound's Confucian ethics of *The Cantos* in the embryonic form. Albright argued:

> Instead of a plan, Pound devised a strategy for creating a self-scrutinizing text, continually extending itself, ramifying outward, as it groped to comprehend its own prior meanings, to improvise new networks of connection, and to assimilate new material: a text shaped like a developing brain. New Cantos form themselves out of schemes to make sense of old Cantos: so the story of *The Cantos* comprises two intertwined stories, one concerning Pound's writing of the poem, the other concerning Pound's interpretations of what he had already written. (Albright, 2001: 59)

Albright's argument offers a clue to the author's conclusion that Pound's Confucianism in later cantos is an interpretation and explanation of what has been presented in Canto XIII.

Eliot's question "what does Mr. Pound believe" began the second period of Pound's Confucianism. Pound's answer in 1934 was concise and confirmative: "I believe the *Ta Hio*." (*LE* 86) What intrigued Pound was the Confucian order in the book — establishing the inner order and then spreading it to the outside society. The oath of his belief pushed Pound to the second step in his serious study of Confucianism. Around the year of 1935, he started to learn Chinese characters so as to be able to study the original texts of Confucian scriptures. His Chinese learning contributed to more Confucian translations and direct quotations of Confucian doctrines or Chinese characters in his poetic and prose writings. Besides his English translations of excerpts from *Lun Yu* (1937), Pound retranslated *Da Xue* (1941, 1942) into Italian, and offered a fresh Italian translation of another Chinese classic — *Zhong Yong* (*The Unwobbling Pivot*, 1945) (he was isolated from English-speaking countries). The poems he composed in this phase, particularly the "China Cantos" and Canto XLIX (also called "The Seven Lakes Canto"), were replete with Confucian ideas. His prose and broadcasts abounded with re-interpretations of Confucian doctrines and such re-interpretations were often manifested in his political views of this period.

At the end of World War II, Pound came to the third stage of his Confucian exploration and also the third serious Confucian study. His incarceration cut him off from the chaotic world and his controversial political condition, and the confinement offered him a tranquil setting to explore the essence of the Confucian classics. Pound's post-war cantos were marked with a grueling spiritual quest, which made them quite different from the cantos he wrote during the 1930s and the early 1940s — replete with political and economic reformation. Besides explicitly expressing his Confucian ideas with copious quotations from Confucian texts, Pound committed himself to a systematic and complete Confucian translation in this period. During the gray years in Washington D. C., he published his English translation of *Da Xue* (1947) and *Zhong Yong* (1947) — both were translated during the dark days at the American Discipline Training Center (DTC) near Pisa, and *Lun Yu* (1951). The first three of the "Four Books" were later published in one volume with the title *Confucius: The Unwobbling Pivot, The Great Digest and The Analects*. As for *Meng Zi*, Pound translated four chapters of Book One into English and published them in 1947. Additionally, Pound translated *Shi Jing* into English and published it with the title *Shih-ching: The Classics Anthology Defined by Confucius* (1954).

Pound's great project was to cure the Western disease with Confucianism. Considering the alienated West, or to be specific, Western "moral obtuseness", Pound immersed himself in Confucianism to cope with Western problems. As a Chinese, rereading his Confucian translations, poetry, prose and etc., the author could not but admire Pound's penetrating insight into the modern society and his prophetic vision of reiterating the modern values of Confucianism to deal with modern problems. His Confucian medicine heals the modern West in three ways: his ideas on man and self, his ethics on man and society, as well as his ethics on man and nature.

Part II Pound's Confucianism

"As working hypothesis say that Kung is superior to Aristotle by totalitarian instinct. His thought is never something scaled off the surface of facts. It is root volition branching out, the ethical weight is present in every phrase." (*GK* 279)

3. Pound's Ideas on Man and Self

3.1 Pound's *Zhi Ren* 知人

In 1938, Pound published one of his "stimulating books" *Guide to Kulchur* in which "he (Pound) covers the whole territory of 'kulchur' — from the Chinese philosophers to the modern poetry, from music to economics"①. In the same year, Pound published his significant Confucian essay "Mang Tsze: The ethics of Mencius" in which he started to use Chinese ideograms increasingly since the first Chinese character *xin* 信 appeared at the end of Canto XXXIV and his beloved Confucian doctrine *zheng ming* 正名 at the end of Canto LI. Even his oft-advocated Confucian term *zheng ming* appeared only once in "Mang Tsze" and just twice in his book *Guide to Kulchur.* However, Pound quoted the ideogram *zhi ren* 知人 seven times in this book, which enjoyed superiority to the other quoted characters because all the other characters appeared no more than twice in this book. It is incredible that such frequently-recurring characters do not arouse the attention of some of the main Poundian-Confucian scholars, such as Mary P. Cheadle and Feng Lan.

The author contends, however, that the seemingly insignificant Chinese characters *zhi ren* 知人 started Pound's real exploration of humanist ideology and deep contemplation of human nature. They appear three times just in the first essay "DIGEST OF THE ANALECTS that is, of the Philosophic Conversations", and the author will start to argue from the second quotation:

> *Humanity? is to love men.*
> *Knowledge, to know men.*
> It is written: Fan-tchi did not understand what Kung meant by these answers.
>
> 知
> 人 (*GK* 18)

This philosophic conversation comes from *Lun Yu* XII. 22 where a Confucian disciple

① The quotation is from the back cover of Pound's *Guide to Kulchur*.

Fan Chi 樊迟 asked Confucius what *ren* 仁 was and what *zhi* 知 was, and Confucius gave him a concise answer, but Fan Chi couldn't understand the rich meanings inhabited in that answer. As a matter of fact, this quotation appeared first in a pamphlet published in Italian and then in the opening essay of *Guide to Kulchur.*① In his complete translation of *The Analects* (1951), Pound rendered it almost the same as that in 1938, as a result of his years of "digest" of *Lun Yu*.

> Fan Ch'ih asked about humaneness. He said: Love men. Ask about knowledge. He said: To know men.
>
> Fan Ch'ih didn't get as far (see through to the end of that answer). (*Con* 248)

Pound translated *zhi ren* 知人 as "to know men". It's obvious that his translation of *zhi ren* 知人 in *The Analects* is consistent with his early interpretation of the term in *Guide to Kulchur*. In fact, his rendering is more or less divergent from other translations. Burton Watson put it into "understand others"; Ku Hweng-Ming (辜鸿铭)② "understanding men"; D. C. Lau (刘殿爵)③ "know your fellow men". Comparing the different translations, Pound's rendering of *ren* 人 is close to that of D. C. Lau who translated *Tao Te Ching*, *Mencius* and *The Analects*. Pound's rendering probably depended on James Legge, whose bilingual editions of the Confucian classics were frequently consulted by Pound when he translated *Lun Yu*.

> Fan Ch'ih asked about benevolence. The Master said, 'It is to love *all* men.' He asked about knowledge. The Master said, 'It is to know *all* men.'
>
> Fan Ch'ih did not immediately understand *these answers*. (Legge, 2009: 260-261)

Ignoring the different translations of *ren* 仁 temporarily and Pound's economical use of words, we find that Pound omitted "*all*" italicized by Legge for emphasis. Zhu Xi 朱熹 (Chu Hsi) explained *bu zhi ren* 不知人 as "the inability to distinguish between

---

① This is borrowed from Cheadle's *Ezra Pound's Confucian Translations* (1997: 116), which originally comes from Gallup's *Ezra Pound, a Bibliography*, no. A44.

② Ku Hweng-Ming (Gu Hongming, 1857-1928) was a Chinese man of letters. He learned a wide range of Chinese philosophy and western science, and was proficient in English, French, German, Latin, Greek, Malaya and other nine languages. He translated three of China's "Four Books" — *Lun Yu*, *Zhong Yong* and *Da Xue*.

③ D. C. Lau (Liu Dianjue, 1921-2010) was a Chinese sinologist and author of the widely read translations of *Tao Te Ching*, *Mencius* and *The Analects*. See https://en.wikipedia.org/wiki/D._C._Lau [2019-06-17].

right and wrong or between good and evil" (朱熹, 2011: 54)[①]. Pound's translation of the doctrine "不患人之不己知，患不知人也" goes as follows: "Not worried that men do not know me, but that I do not understand men." (*Con* 197) "Knowledge is to know men." — Pound asserted this through the book *Guide to Kulchur*. But "to know men" didn't mean the study of anthropology. Pound stated: "If you translate him (Mr. Alexander Pope), the proper study of man is anthropology, you get nearer the source of error." (*GK* 99) *Zhi ren*, to some degree, becomes an ethical term containing a moral understanding of Confucianism. The simple and straightforward translation of "to know men" contains profound meanings in three aspects: to know others as Burton Watson's rendering, to know self, and to know human nature which is *ren xing* 人性 in Chinese. To know others is a superficial meaning that Pound has explicitly referred to in *Guide to Kulchur*; to know what makes man is significant for Pound, and more importantly, it is an essential prerequisite for knowing self.

Pound's simple and superficial understanding of *zhi ren* as "to know others" initiated his interpretation of the two Chinese characters. He inserted the two characters in English texts for the first time after his recording of an anecdote from *The Analects*:

> May we not suppose that the answers in XIV, 10 of the Analects have been treasured as examples that Kung employed the right word neither in excess nor less than his meaning?
>
> 知
> 人 (*GK* 18)

It's about *Lun Yu* XIV. 10, in which someone asked Confucius what kinds of person Zi Chan 子产 (Pound's Tze-Chan), Zi Xi 子西 (Pound's Tze-Hsi) and Guan Zhong 管仲 (Pound's Kwan Chung) were, respectively. Pound recorded it in his complete translation of *The Analects*:

> Someone asked about (this) Tze-Chan. He said: A kind man.
> Asked about Tze-Hsi. He said: That bloke! That one!
> Asked about Kwan Chung. He said: *Jen yeh*, … (*Con* 256)

① Zhu Xi annotated "*bu huan ren zhi bu ji zhi, huan bu zhi ren ye* 不患人之不己知，患不知人也" (*Lun Yu* I.16), in which he explained "*bu zhi ren, ze shi fei xie zheng huo bu neng bian* 不知人，则是非邪正或不能辩". Namely, *bu zhi ren* means the inability to distinguish between right and wrong or between good and evil.

The master simply commented Guan Zhong as *ren ye* 人也 (Pound's Jen yeh) which might mean *ren* 人 with the virtue of *ren* 仁. In his essay, Pound lauded Confucius for employing the right word, implying his compliment of Confucius's right judgment of persons.

Pound's interpretation is not groundless and baseless because *zhi ren* always implies that the lord or king is so capable of knowing persons with *ren* 仁 that he employs them to help him govern the state. People eulogize such a wise emperor with an idiomatic expression *zhi ren shan ren* 知人善任 meaning "to know one's subordinates well enough to assign them jobs commensurate with their abilities".[①] In XII. 22 of *Lun Yu*, Zi Xia 子夏 (Pound's Tse-Hsia) reinterpreted *zhi ren* to Fan Chi by giving examples to explain *zhi ren shan ren.* Pound expressed the complicated philosophical implication of *zhi ren* in this way: "Shun had the Empire, picked out Kao-Yao from the multitude, promoted him, and wrong 'uns departed. T'ang had the Empire, he picked out I Yin from all the hordes, promoted him, and the wrong 'uns departed." (*Con* 248) Lao Tsu made an inspiring statement on knowing others and self: "A man who knows others is wise, while a man who knows himself is wiser."[②]

Apart from "to know others", Pound annexed insightful annotations to *zhi ren* — knowing what a man was or why a man was called a man rather than a mammal, which was well manifested in his interpretation of *ren* 仁. Pound considered *ren* 仁 as the pivot point of Confucian teachings in his early academic years, and his translation of *ren* is notably consistent in his Confucian translations. According to Cheadle (1997: 90), Pound consulted Morrison's dictionary and followed Pauthier's translation rather than James Legge's rendering of *ren* 仁 as benevolence. In his 1928 version of *Da Xue*, *ren* 仁 is translated as "the practice of the humanities" or "humanity". In the opening terminology section of the 1969 *Confucius*, Pound offered an elaborate definition of *ren* 仁: "*Humanituas*, humanity, in the full sense of the word, 'manhood.' The man and his full contents." (*Con* 22) Pound frequently used "humanity" or "humaneness" to refer to this term, indicating that Pound's *ren* 仁 refers to "the totality of inner human personality" (Lan, 2005: 88) or "a kind of individual completeness and integrity" (Cheadle, 1997: 90).

---

① This translation is from the web-edition of *The New Chinese-English Dictionary*. See http://dict.youdao.com/w/%E7%9F%A5%E4%BA%BA%E5%96%84%E4%BB%BB/.

② The quotation is from XXXIII of Lao Tsu's *Tao Te Ching* (老子, 2011: 87). The Chinese version is "知人者智，自知者明" and the English translation is as in the above text.

Pound caught the core of Confucianism — *ren* 仁 during his early years of Confucian study. In Canto XIII, the idea of *ren* 仁 was exemplified by several anecdotes. Among them lies one, which always arouses debates in Confucians:

> And they said: If a man commit murder
> Should his father protect him, and hide him?
> And Kung said;
> He should hide him. (Canto XIII 59)

The father and the son hide defects of each other. "Uprightness" and sincerity lie in such conduct. Gu Sou (瞽瞍, Shun's father) was assumed to kill a person. What would Shun do? Protect him or sentence the old man to death? Neither. Shun would give up the throne, save his father from the jail, flee to a remote coastal hut and live there with his father forever. The love for his father was overwhelming everything (朱熹, 2011: 137). Rectitude consists in the instinct of love for clan relatives, and Pound later wrote it in *The Pisan Cantos*. The nature of *ren* 仁 was "to love men" as Pound interpreted, especially to love clan relatives. Pound's choice of this episode gave evidence of his catching the nature of *ren* 仁 because Confucius regarded *qin qin* 亲亲 as the starting point of *ren* 仁. Therefore, kindred love drives a son to save his father instinctively, and the act that a father keeps his son from harm is reasonable and acceptable because it's the father's duty to protect the son.

Pound's choice of anecdotes related directly or indirectly to Confucius is not random but discreet. The next two anecdotes indicate Confucius's criterion of good persons or real men who possess the personality of *ren* 仁. An individual, according to Confucius, should be judged by the true nature of his personality rather than by his social achievements. A person with *ren* 仁 may be having difficulties and hardly be recognized. That's why Confucius married his daughter to Kong-Tch'ang who "was in prison" and his niece to "Nan-Young who was out of office" (Canto XIII 59). The high premise of *ren* 仁 is to love relatives and respect persons with virtue. "Wang" 王 who "ruled with moderation" and "the prince" who "has gathered about him / All the savants and artists" are emperors who govern their state with *ren* 仁 (Canto XIII 60). As for governing the state, Confucianism lays stress on ruling people through virtues of inner power rather than laws. Furthermore, a person with *ren* 仁 is honest and modest. The honest historians in lines 69-72 contrast sharply with Yuan Rang (原壤, Pound's Yuan Jang) who "sat by the roadside pretending to be receiving wisdom" (Canto XIII 59). Such examples that Pound gleaned from Confucian classics asserted that Pound had discovered the core of Confucianism — *ren* 仁 at the preliminary stage of his involvement in Confucianism.

In the mid-1930s when Pound started learning Chinese characters, he began to insert the Chinese ideogram 仁 into his English texts, and his understanding of *ren* 仁 was extended. He input 仁 into his English texts around the year of 1938 in the prose "Mang Tsze" and the book *Guide to Kulchur*. 仁, "the ideogram for ARETE" (*SP* 89), is interpreted or defined as "the whole man and the whole man's contents" (*SP* 85) and "entire man" (*SP* 89). Pound fully contemplated *ren* 仁 during his confined days at the DTC near Pisa and St. Elizabeths Hospital of Washington D.C. His comprehensive understanding of the Confucian doctrine is handsomely reflected in his ample quotations of the ideogram 仁 and 人, his repeated references to *si duan* 四端, and his direct expression of "the humane man", namely "*humanitas*".

Pound's understanding of *ren* 仁 is well manifested in his translation *ren zhe ai ren* 仁者爱人 (humanity is to love men). In the Confucian moral philosophy, the concept of *ren* 仁 as an ethical idea was established by Confucius himself. Mencius inherited the basic idea of Confucius's *ren* 仁 and developed it to *si duan* 四端. Mencius's formulation of *si duan* refers to four ethical potential characters: *ren* 仁 (humaneness, benevolence), *yi* 义 (righteousness), *li* 礼 (propriety, the rites), and *zhi* 智 (wisdom). "According to Mencius, these innate capacities are not instilled into us from without but are part of us when we are born." (Lan, 2005: 151) In their natural state, each of these beginnings is an innate sense constituting the heart/mind (*xin* 心). *Ren* 仁 is manifested as the sense of compassion (sympathy with the suffering of others, for instance), *yi* as the sense of shame, *li* as the sense of respect, and *zhi* as the sense of right and wrong. The purpose of self-development is to cultivate these innate senses and compassion. In Mencius's formulation of *si duan*, *ren* 仁 serves as the sense of compassion towards one's fellow human beings. Pound's understanding of *The Analects* — "Humanity? (is) to love men" exposed his early keen awareness of the essence of the ethical implication of *ren* 仁. Therefore, Pound's comprehension of *ren* 仁 began with his understanding of *The Analects* and expanded after his reading of Mencius's formulation of *si duan*.

The doctrine of *si duan* 四端 (Pound's poetic tuan) forms an important and recurrent theme in *The Cantos*, emerging in various forms (Canto LXXXVI 581; Canto LXXXIX 621; Canto XCIX 720, 731; Canto CIX 792). Pound named *duan* 端 as "tuan" or "foundations" in the epic and "origins" in his Confucian translations (*Con* 119). In Canto LXXXV, Pound expressed *si duan* in the following form:

THE FOUR TUAN[1]

端

or foundations (Canto LXXXV 565)

He gave poetic expression to the innate personality of human beings shortly in Canto XCIX.

The basis is man,
and the rectification of officers
but the four TUAN
are from nature
jen, i, li, chih
Not from descriptions in the school house; (Canto XCIX 731)

Pound asserted the four TUAN (jen, i, li, chih) were from nature. Here Pound's concept of "nature" referred not to the natural world but to "the inborn nature" of man (*Con* 99) because he subsequently argued that human beings couldn't obtain these foundational dispositions, which were naturally endowed from outside like school teaching.

Pound presented *ren* 仁 as the core of Confucianism in *The Cantos*. *Ren* 仁 is the primary Confucian virtue and also the first of *si tuan*. Pound clearly and for the first time stated that Confucian humanism was composed of "THE FOUR TUAN" in Canto LXXXV:

Have scopes and beginnings tchōung
仁 智 chèu
Jen[2] chih[4] i-li
are called chung[1-4]
衷
仁 好 *(1508, Mathews)* (Canto LXXXV 564)

This stanza can be interpreted in two ways. Firstly, Pound attached importance to *ren* 仁 and *zhi* 智 among the four dispositions because the two Chinese characters were chosen by Pound to be inserted in the English text. *Ren* 仁 bears more importance because it appears twice in the short stanza and ends with "仁 好" (literally *ren* 仁 is good). Secondly, *zhong* 衷 (Pound's chung), according to Cookson (2001: 172), is "inner nature; the heart instilled with the above virtues". To be exact, the heart instilled with *ren* 仁, *yi* 义, *li* 礼 and *zhi* 智 (Pound's "Jen^2 chih^4 i-li") is *zhong* 衷. The visual effect of the poetic lines is that 衷 stands exactly in the middle, which represents another Chinese character *zhong* 中. Pound maintained: "It is hard to stand firm in the middle." (Canto XIII 59) Therefore, for Pound, a man with the virtues of *ren*, *yi*, *li* and *zhi*, is finally assured to "stand firmly in the middle".

"To know men", or to know human nature is the basic step to know self, as Pound phrased it in "Sophist" — "to know thyself" (*GK* 79). The notion of "to know thyself" is closely related to Pound's ideology of individualists. As discussed earlier, Pound's concern with individualist philosophy started in the early years of his poetic career. In a 1911 poem "Rendondillas", Pound announced a manifesto of self: "I sing of the special case, / The truth is the individual" (*CEP* 219, 221). In Pound's early works, he always reiterated the "rights of man" (*SR* 176). In his study on Gourmont (1920), he compared Gourmont's idea on individual rights to Confucius's:

> He (Gourmont) recognizes the right of individuals to *feel* differently. Confucian, Epicurean, a considerer and entertainer of ideas, this complicated sensuous wisdom is almost the one ubiquitous element, the "self" which keeps his superficially heterogeneous work vaguely "unified". (*LE* 340-341)

Perhaps it's the Confucian respect for the individuals that brought Pound to Confucian works. In a 1917 essay with the title "Provincialism the enemy", Pound endorsed Confucianism decisively because of its great respect for "the value of personality", openly condemning the forces of "provincialism" that always tried "to control the acts of other people" and to "coerce others into uniformity" (*SP* 193, 189).

"To know thyself" becomes a slogan in Pound's individualist humanity. Then what does "self" mean? Self, "as a cultural product", differs across two cultural contexts — Pound's native culture, i.e. the North American culture, and the Chinese traditional culture represented by Confucianism. Heine (2001: 881-905) made an elaborate "examination of East Asian and North American selves". A widely accepted fact is that the American culture values "a rather extreme case of individualism" as Heine posited that "the United States was founded on an ideology that emphasizes the importance of self-determination and individual rights" (Heine, 2001: 884). The American self values independence while the East Asian self (or to be specific, the

Confucian self) "is typically described as being collectivistic or interdependent, reflecting the significant role of relationships with ingroup members in the construction of the self" (Heine, 2001: 885). "In particular," he added, "this interdependence is shaped by their common Confucian heritage." The Confucian self is interdependent, but Heine (2001: 894-895) argued that "the interdependent self cannot be interdependent with everyone". It means that one should gain the ability to be independent as a sole being, and then one can be accepted as an ingroup member. "Gaining admission into the sacrosanct ingroup is a substantial accomplishment, and these relationships should hold a privileged position for East Asian selves...harmony is maintained when individuals fulfill obligations to others." (Heine, 2001: 895) To put it succinctly, only when individuals "fulfill obligations" and duties to others can the self enjoys "a privileged position" in a community. In this way, Pound's early articulation of his belief — "dependence on self is the core of Confucian philosophy"① does not contravene the Confucian "interdependent self". Both Pound's discovery of "dependence on self" and Heine's discussion of "gaining admission into the sacrosanct ingroup" indicate an understanding of Confucian cultivation — establishing the order within the self.

Besides cultural views of self, independence and interdependence, the psychological processes of self-enhancement and self-criticism are also important because they participate in the making of self (Kitayama et al., 1997). The Western self is characterized by a self-enhancing motivation, which means viewing self positively. In contrast, East Asians tend to evaluate themselves less positively than North Americans, and show little evidence of self-enhancing biases (Heine, 2001: 899). This orientation is termed self-criticism. They must become vigilant to any shortcomings indicated where they need to make more efforts to better fulfill their roles (Heine, 2001: 898). This shows that East Asians value effort and are liable to examine themselves when they give a poor performance and obtain unsatisfactory achievements. Such findings meet Pound's slogan "Missing the bull's eye seeks the cause in himself" (Makin, 2005: 177)②.

---

① In the 1914 essay "The words of Ming Mao", Pound articulated his belief that "dependence on self is the core of Confucian philosophy". According to Zhaoming Qian and Feng Lan, it is considered as the first and earliest Confucian article so far. See Qian (2006: 157-177) and Lan (2004: 79-89).

② It was used by Pound as a flyer passed on walls during the war, and was one of the three main references in Pound's article introducing Confucius to Italian readers in 1941 (*Con* 127; Carpenter, 1988: 635).

As for Pound's ideology of self or individualist, Lan attributed it to Western individualism totally and absolutely. He argued: "Pound's individual agenda rests on the concept of the autonomous or sovereign individual, a notion central to the entire tradition of Western individualism" and continued to maintain that Pound's individual ideology was shown in "three fundamental rights of the individual: freedom, privacy, and self-development" (Lan, 2005: 94). As Heine (2001: 884) contended, "understanding the self requires an understanding of the culture that sustains it". The author argues that both the North American culture, which bred young Pound, and the Confucian heritage to which he gave a career-long devotion should be taken into consideration when Pound's ideology on self is under discussion. Taking account of the two dramatically divergent cultures in which Pound was involved, the author holds that Pound's ideology on self is complicated and sometimes perplexing because the Eastern Confucian self and the Western individual self, somehow, have merged in him. Pound's self involves self-enhancement as well as self-criticism, and entails the unity of inner self / internal self and outer self / external self, or the private self and the public self. The self in Confucianism is essentially an ethical concept, representing a holistic view of humanhood and a continuingly constructive process driven by self-cultivation and moral orientations (Yao, 1996: 179).

The Confucian self and the entire tradition of Western individualism are synthesized in Pound's quest of the psyche. Pound's self-enhancing motivation is well reflected in his translation of an important Confucian doctrine *ke ji fu li* 克己复礼. One of Confucius's disciples, Yan Yuan 颜渊, once asked the master what consisted in *ren* 仁 and how to achieve it. Confucius answered in a celebrated way and Pound put it into a kind of "Song of Myself" in English①:

> Support oneself and return to the rites, that makes a man. If a man can be adequate to himself for one day and return to the rites, the empire would come home to its manhood. This business of manhood sprouts from oneself, how can it sprout from others? (*Con* 243)
>
> *Ke ji fu li wei ren. Yi ri ke ji fu li, tian xia gui Ren yan. Wei Ren you ji, er you hu ren zai.* 克己复礼为仁。一日克己复礼，天下归仁焉。为仁由己，而由乎人哉？(*Lun Yu* XII. 1)

Pound's translation diverged from his "cribs" — James Legge's bilingual editions of the classics to which Pound always referred during that period:

① Lan (2005: 85) made a detailed analysis of Pound's translation of *ke ji fu li* (克己复礼).

> To subdue one's self and return to propriety, is perfect virtue. If a man can for one day subdue himself and return to propriety, all under heaven will ascribe perfect virtue to him. Is the practice of perfect virtue from a man himself, or is it from others? (Legge, 2009: 250)

In the comparison of Pound's translation with Legge's, two significant differences are easily found. First is the different striking translations of 克己. Pound's "support oneself" sharply contrasts with Legge's "subdue one's self" which indicates an opposite attitude to self. The next difference rests on the different translations of the last sentence. Pound's translation not only exactly delivers the meaning, but also closely follows a Chinese sentence pattern — a rhetorical question. It's conspicuous that the business of manhood sprouts from oneself rather than from others. But Legge's translation makes it a real question implying an alternative choice of the two parts. Namely, to be "from a man himself" or to be "from others", that's a question.

Pound's unique translation of *ke ji* 克己 as "support oneself" marks a remarkable difference with the Western translations either before or after him. Pauthier (observed "avoir un empire absolu sur soi-même" (have absolute self-control),① Chan "master oneself",② Lau "overcoming the self",③ and Roger Ames "self-discipline".④ Lan (2005: 86) made an elaborate discussion of the historical evolution of the interpretation of 克己 in Chinese Confucian scholarship and drew a conclusion that Pound's translation of *ke ji* served as supporting the self resonates with that of Zhi Li (1527-1602) and Yizhi Fang (1611-1671). But "there is no evidence that Pound ever read these writers" and "Pound's interpretation is based on his own understanding of Confucian ideas about human nature" (Lan, 2005: 88). Lan's argumentation is very persuasive. What the author wants to add is that Pound's "self-supporting" view indicated by his *ke ji* translation is influenced by his native culture advocating self-enhancement.

---

① See Pauthier, *Confucius et Mencius*, 178. He translated the Confucian classic *Confucius et Mencius: Les Quatre Livres de Philosophie Morale et Politique de la Chine.* Pound's first translation of *Da Xue* was based on Pauthier's Confucian version.

② See Chan, *A Source Book in Chinese Philosophy*, 38.

③ See Lau, *The Analects*, 203. "If for a single day a man could return to the observance of the rites through overcoming himself, then the whole Empire would consider benevolence to be his."

④ See Ames, *The Analects of Confucius*, 152. "Through self-discipline and observing ritual propriety (*li* 礼) one becomes authoritative in one's conduct." Some of the notes are borrowed from Lan's *Ezra Pound and Confucianism — Remaking Humanism in the Face of Modernity* (Toronto, Buffalo and London: University of Toronto Press, 2005: 213-214)

3.2 Pound's Self-cultivation

Pound presumed that the valuable point of the Confucian self was based on Confucian ethics, and its beauty was that it had a clear division between the private self and the public self or the internal self and the external self.① However, the problems of American life and American people were that most people couldn't distinguish between what's the private self and what's the public self. Pound once dreadfully regretted:

> The drear horror of American life can be traced to two damnable roots, or perhaps it is only one root: 1. The loss of *all* distinction between public and private affairs. 2. The tendency to mess into other people's affairs before establishing order in one's own affairs, and in one's own thought...The principle of good is enunciated by Confucius; it consists in establishing order within oneself. This order or harmony spreads by a sort of contagion without specific effort. The principle of evil consists in messing into other people's affairs. (*SP* 216)

Confucianism, by contrast, advocates respect for personality and self-cultivation.

> The thought is for the community. Confucius' constant emphasis is on the value of personality, on the outlines of personality, on the man's right to preserve the outlines of his personality, and of his duty not to interfere with the personalities of others. (*SP* 193)

What Pound repeatedly stressed was that one shouldn't interfere in others' lives but focus on his or her own life and cultivate himself or herself to be a proper person.

The inner self or the private self is frequently advocated by Pound and reflected in his interpretation of *cheng* 诚 which is also a crucial step on the way to being self-cultivated. Pound expounded extensively on the concept of *cheng* deriving from the doctrine of *cheng yi* 诚意. The concept of *cheng*, occupying an important place in both Confucian metaphysics and ethics, constitues a major theme in the Confucian

① The Confucian self is well-discussed by Yao. According to Yao (1996: 184), "Confucian ethics grounds the self in the unity between one's private self and the public self in the practical process, especially in the unity between mind and body, between one's internal or private aspect and one's external or public aspect, and between the self-appreciation and the other-judgments. In this unity, the others' reactions to, and perceptions of, the self are not taken to be merely an imagined 'mirror' to reflect one's true self, nor to be the 'masks' to cover one's real identity, but the important part of one's identity and the content of the self as real and actual as one's own perceptions".

classic *Zhong Yong* which posits *cheng* as a key point to realize *zhong yong zhi dao* 中庸之道. Pound's persistent reading of *cheng* from *Da Xue* through *Zhong Yong* indicates he was aware that *cheng* in Confucianism was, first of all, an ethical category. Pound sometimes followed James Legge's translation of *cheng* as "sincerity" which, however, differed from Legge's understanding of the word in Christian ethics. He defined *cheng* in the terminology preceding the 1969 *Confucius*: "诚 'Sincerity'. The precise definition of the word, pictorially the sun's lance coming to rest on the precise spot verbally. The righthand half of this compound means: to perfect, bring to focus." (*Con* 20) Such a pictographic interpretation conveys two meanings: First of all, sincerity is a synonymous term with linguistic precision, as Lan (2005: 71) discussed; second, *cheng* is to "perfect, bring to focus" showing a kind of instruction to realize *ren* 仁 and *zhong yong zhi dao* 中庸之道. Pound also roughly defined *cheng* as "not lying to oneself" (*Con* 47), bearing a rich ethical meaning. The simple definition is close to the word "honesty" or "candor".

Pound's reading of *cheng* does not contradict the interpretations of major Confucian exegetes since neo-Confucianism. For example, *cheng* was interpreted by Zhu Xi as "reality, truth, and freedom from error".① Modern commentators, like Weiming Tu (1989: 73), read *cheng* as "a principle of subjectivity" by which a person can become "true" to himself and "form a unity with Heaven". With them, Pound shared the recognition that *cheng* refers to a dynamic process whereby the individual mind is able to complete knowledge of reality. We come to see how Pound envisioned the role of precise language in relation to three aspects of cognition: reconciling the human mind and the transcendental mind, prescribing the procedure of self-actualization, and clarifying the truth of things obtained from observation of nature (Lan, 2005: 71).

"Not lying to oneself", as Pound's simple definition of *cheng* indicates to be a real and true self, implies "the idea of self-knowledge: of awareness of one's self and of its real intentions — to be distinguished, for example, from selves and intentions one would like to have, or would like to persuade other people that one has" (Makin, 2005: 173). One's real intention, in other words, is the voice from the "inner self". Makin (2005: 193) held that "the *cheng* of the *Great Learning*, the *Doctrine of the Mean*, and the *Mencius*...posits something outside one's immediate thoughts in the sense that, at any particular moment, it is already there, it is complex, and it needs to

① Zhu Xi interpreted "诚" as "真实无妄". This is one of the most influential interpretations in Neo-Confucianists of the Song Dynasty.

be searched, acknowledged, and criticized". What Makin maintained was that the "inner self" was always there waiting for us to explore and criticize. Pound's recognition of the "inner self" benefited from his years of reading and contemplating the concept of *cheng* and other related concepts, such as *shen* 慎, *de* 德 and *yi* 意, which will be interpreted shortly in a discussion or self-cultivation.

Self-cultivation (*xiu shen* 修身), in Pound's words, refers to "having order within" the self, which is a constant and life-long quest for the Confucian self. Pound knew the importance of order for a person as well as for the society at the onset of his learning Confucianism. The idea of order was one of the first Confucian principles that came into Pound's mind. In Canto XIII, the words written "on the bo leaves" occupy the center place of the poem:

> And Kung said, and wrote on the bo leaves:
> If a man have not order within him
> He can not spread order about him;
> And if a man have not order within him
> His family will not act with due order;
> And if the prince have not order within him
> He can not put order in his dominions. (Canto XIII 59)

These lines are from the first chapter of *Da Xue* through which Pound strongly believed in the order established by Confucian disciples. When Pound deliberately placed the idea of order in his verse, he probably could not have recognized the difference among Chinese Confucian concepts *qi jia* 齐家, *zhi guo* 治国 and *ping tian xia* 平天下, but surely he captured the core of this Confucian principle because he repeatedly used the word "order" in each line. Using "order" six times was enough to prove that Pound knew the importance of order for a man, a family, a state, and, as well, for the whole society. The ultimate source of order lies in individuals rather than any external forces, and the beauty of the Confucian order rests on the fact that the individual serves as a radiating center in the order of self, family and society. To put it in another way, a harmonious and orderly society depends on men "having order within" themselves. To achieve an order within oneself needs self-cultivation or "self-discipline" (*Con* 31). Pound provided a step-by-step procedure for achieving the order within the self:

> When things had been classified in organic categories, knowledge moved toward

> fulfillment; given the extreme knowledge points, the inarticulate thoughts were defined with precision [the sun's lance coming to rest on the precise spot verbally]. Having attained this precise verbal definition [*aliter*, this sincerity], they then stabilized their hearts, they disciplined themselves. (*Con* 31, 33)

According to the text, self-cultivation, conclusively speaking, goes through a three-step process: extending "knowledge to the utmost" [*zhi zhi* 致知] (*Con* 31), attaining "this precise verbal definition [*aliter*, this sincerity]" [*cheng yi* 诚意], and stabilizing (or rectifying) their hearts [*zheng xin* 正心].

Among the three steps, rectifying the heart is the key to self-cultivation as *Da Xue* instructs. To establish the personal order through self-cultivation, Pound attached special importance to *cheng* 诚, a prerequisite to *zheng xin*. At the same time, "the extreme knowledge", to achieve by classifying things "in organic categories", is the basis of this process. For Pound, as Cheadle (1997: 69) argued, self-discipline "is achieved by a natural or organic organization of perceptions or facts into a system of knowledge, a vocabulary that in turn enables one to 'define one's inarticulate thoughts precisely'". Therefore, *cheng* and knowledge, in Pound's view, are two essential and inevitable steps to achieve self-cultivation.

Pound interpreted *cheng* 诚 in a variety of ways. The earliest *cheng* in "Mang Tsze" (1938) is "the *word* and the action of fixing or *perfecting*", in which he grasped two keywords "word" and "action". Analyzed pictographically, the left side of the compound "诚", namely "讠" (言), is simply the sign for "word". As for the right-hand half of "诚", Pound saw "the actions of *perfecting*" through the ideogram "成", which exactly coincided with the process of Confucian self-cultivation — self-perfection. In the terminology section preceding the 1969 *Confucius*, Pound reiterated that "the righthand half of this compound means: to perfect, bring to focus" (*Con* 20). Moreover, this interpretation of "诚" also indicates Pound's awareness of the consistency of one's words and actions. A couple of years later, he wrote in *The Unwobbling Pivot*: "His words accord with his acts and his conduct." (*Con* 123) In this sense, Pound's interpretation of Confucianism through the Chinese character 诚 coincides with that of the Chinese Confucian philosopher Yangming Wang[①]. One of

① Yangming Wang (1472-1529), whose courtesy name is Bo'an, is a Chinese idealist Neo-Confucian philosopher, official, educationist and general during the Ming Dynasty. He is commonly regarded as the most important Neo-Confucian thinker after Zhu Xi 朱熹.

Wang's significant philosophical ideas is the integration of knowledge and action (*zhi xing he yi* 知行合一).

Yi 意, not separated from *cheng* 诚, is one of Pound's most creative interpretations of an ideogram. It is often rendered simply as "intention". Discovering one's intention becomes Pound's phrase "the inarticulate thoughts [the tones given off by the heart]" (*Con* 51). According to Cheadle (1997: 68), Pound's interpretation is corroborated coincidentally by the sinologist Peter Boodberg, and it is perhaps defined as "THE HEART'S ENTONE" (the heart's inner tone). Pound must have found that the character *yi* 意 composed of two ideograms *yin* 音 (sound or tone) and *xin* 心 (heart) when he tried to interpret the character. Moreover, the sound or tone is posited over the heart; therefore, he concluded "the tones given off by the heart" or "the heart's tone". *Cheng yi* 诚意 in Pound's version is "the precise verbal expression for his inarticulate thoughts" or "the sun's lance falling true on the word, and the heart giving off tone" (*Con* 51). So finding the perfect verbal expression for a real self is what Pound understood as *cheng*.

Cheng is a way to find the inner self because sincerity means "not lying to oneself" or not deceiving oneself. Only in this way can one find the real self. It also advocates a self-critical point of view to examine the self, with which one faces squarely one's own shortcomings and know the real self — "to know thyself" in Pound's maxim. "To know thyself" can also be termed as "self-understanding" or "self-knowledge". "'Understanding the motives of your own acts'," Cheadle (1997: 76) argued, "had been important to Pound as a fundamental of Confucianism since the 1910s, and it remained so." Makin (2005: 177) even heightened Pound's self-knowledge almost the same as *cheng*, and he argued: "Pound repeatedly offered sincerity and self-knowledge as the key to Confucianism."

Self-understanding in the Confucian sense is developed by means of "sincerity" (Cheadle, 1997: 94-95). "Finding the precise word for the inarticulate heart's tone," Pound explained at the beginning of Part Four of *Da Xue*, "means not lying to oneself, as in the case of hating a bad smell or loving a beautiful person, also called respecting one's own nose." (*Con* 47) Therefore, *cheng* basically is the prerequisite to self-knowledge — to know the inner self. Pound's "to know thyself" is merged into the concept of *de* 德 (Pound's *te*): "The 'know thyself' carried into actions. Said action also serving to clarify the self knowledge." (*Con* 21) "Pound's interpretation of 德 is close to Boodberg's," Cheadle (1997: 287) argued, "but turns Boodberg's notion of a sort of introverted 'moral uprighting' into an extroverted 'action' that results from that internal moral discipline." In *The Cantos*, Pound wrote:

> But if you will follow this process
> 德
> not a lot of signs, but the one sign
> etctera
> plus always Τέχνη
> and from Τέχνη back to σεαυτόν (Canto LXXXV 566)

For a great person, a king or an emperor, what you need to do is to follow just this virtue of *de* 德 "not a lot of sings". "But the one sign" is enough. What you should do more is to learn Τέχνη (craft or "skill in making things") and move from skill back to σεαυτόν (oneself).① Pound's Τέχνη (skill), to some degree, is knowledge. From knowledge back to oneself emphasizes the process of "seeing clearly into himself and thereby directing his acts" (*Con* 133). *De* 德 is exemplary of Shun: "Shun in knowing himself, he was a sage and he acted on the clarity of his self-knowledge." (*Con* 133) Only those who have "this capacity for seeing clearly into himself and thereby directing his acts" can perforce come to the throne, and have high honors, the enduring fame and longevity (*Con* 133).

Pound placed great emphasis on this Confucian doctrine: "If a man does not discipline himself he cannot bring order into the home…To govern a state one must first bring order into one's family." (*Con* 57) With these cardinal points of *Da Xue*, Pound intended to stress sorting out your own (national) house and only afterwards concerning yourself with sorting out others. The sharp difference between Confucianism and Christianity rests on this, which is well manifested in the Bridson interview:

> Bridson: I asked Pound how he felt that Confucianism differed from Christianity. His reply amused me.
>
> Pound: Well I made a definition early in life and I found that I could always get a favorable response from the Afro-American colleagues-in-misfortune at the bughouse. In contrast to Confucianism, doesn't Christianity boil itself down to one commandment,

---

① The Greek words Τέχνη and σεαυτόν mean "skill in making things" and "oneself", respectively. See Terrell's *A Companion to the Cantos of Ezra Pound* (1993: 470).

> namely, "Thou shalt attend to thy neighbor's business before thou attendest to thine own?" ("Interview" 178)①

Pound's response in the Bridson's interview resonates with the 1917 criticism upon Christianity in "Imaginary Letters VII": "Thou shalt attend to thy neighbour's business in preference to thine own." (*PD* 71) Actually, in his works, Pound ceaselessly denounced the person who made trouble by exporting his own problem because he set out to find errors of his fellow men rather than to sort out his own inner problems. Confucianism, in stark contrast, advocates "missing the bull's eye the cause in himself" (*Con* 127). In other words, for the Confucian self, self-analysis and self-criticism should be the first concern for a man. But the basis, in any case, is self-knowledge: a real understanding of your own "house", of your own self. The phrase "started from himself, and made perfection" (Froula, 1983: 74) is Pound's early discovery. Pound valued self-knowledge as the most fundamental of Confucian virtues.

The next step, after *cheng* 诚, is to study the extension of "knowledge to the utmost" (*zhi zhi* 致知), which is the basis of self-cultivation. "This completion of knowledge" is achieved by "sorting things into organic categories", which is Pound's translation of *ge wu* 格物. *Ge wu* means "the study of the nature of things" or "the study of the phenomena of nature", which is, according to Zhu (2005: 60), an archaic word for "natural science" in Chinese. This explanation is based on the traditional Chinese understanding of *ge wu*: a natural way to know the organic world — to observe nature and find out the principles of nature so as to get along with nature. It tells us that knowledge is to learn from nature and respect the laws of nature. However, knowledge means more than that for Pound. If *ge wu*, "natural science" as Zhu referred to, is the knowledge that is required for a profound person, Pound accentuated another kind of knowledge which could be defined as "human science".

It's time to return back to *zhi zhe zhi ren* 知者知人. Pound's translation mainly followed Legge's bilingual translations. Interestingly enough, Legge wrote "ABOUT BENEVOLENCE AND WISDOM; — HOW KNOWLEDGE SUBSERVES BENEVOLENCE" as his exegesis at the footnote of the same page of his translation (Legge, 2009: 260). It proves that Legge's rendering 知 as "knowledge" rather than "wisdom" does not result from his ignorance, but ascribes to a kind of purposeful choice. Although there are some over-lapping in the meanings of the two words

① It's an indirect quotation from Makin's "Pound, Confucian sincerity, and America" (2005: 181-182).

"wisdom" and "knowledge", it's not difficult to find that "wisdom" stresses "the ability to use your knowledge", while "knowledge" attaches importance to "learning" or "study", namely *xue* 学 in Chinese.[①] Legge chose the word "knowledge" in his version because he intended to emphasize the importance of learning. Pound must have noticed the two interpretations of *zhi* 知 when he read Legge's translation. He deliberately followed Legge to render *zhi* 知 as "knowledge" despite "a persistent resistance to that influence" of his predecessors (Lan, 2005: 27). Pound didn't completely follow Legge. Besides the different translations of 仁, another great difference exists in Pound's omitting the italic "*all*". Pound repeatedly wrote in his book *Guide to Kulchur* that "knowledge is to know men" (*GK* 17, 18, 98, 122, 124) rather than "knowledge is to know *all* men".

Now that Pound translated *zhi* 知 as "knowledge", it's necessary to make it clear — what did knowledge mean for Pound. Pound contended that knowledge came from life and at the same time guided life. "Real knowledge goes into natural man in tidbits. A scrap here, a scrap there; always pertinent, linked to safety, or nutrition or pleasure." (*GK* 99) Sometimes real knowledge would be recorded or reflected with written words or in the form of poetry. Poetry could be good or bad, and real knowledge should be in the form of good poetry. He once deplored: "But nice men dislike bad poetry. Ho yuss! Vurry true / 知人. " (*GK* 122)

Not all literati or philosophers were capable of providing "real knowledge" for human beings. Pound denied that Kant and Calvin had the ability to teach people real knowledge for he stated: "Somewhere about here we hump into Kant and Calvin, and somewhere, in the lines preceding, we slip out of 知人." (*GK* 124)

"Classics" contains rich sources of knowledge and wisdom but not all "classics" do so. Pound criticized modern universities because they "have given NO thought whatever to adjusting curricula so as to include and/or prefer the best available 'classics'" (*GK* 314). After the quotation of 知人 in this part, he compared the classics of Aristotle and Kung: "Aristotle preaches the doctrine of the mean. Kung, however, of the mean that stands fast." (*GK* 314-315) He also argued that Aristotle's Nicomache was not real ethics. "The Nicomachean treatise…was composed during a decadence, the greeks had already collapsed. Conscious or unconscious subversivism." (*GK* 314-315) But Kung and Dante "have a much firmer hold on the real, and a much deeper *intendimento*" (*GK* 317). Pound asserted: "A REAL book is one whose words

① The comparison of the two words "wisdom" and "knowledge" is based on explanations from the web-edition of *Longman Dictionary Of Contemporary English* and *Cambridge Dictionary of American English.*

grow even luminous as one's own experience increases or as one is led or edged over into considering them with greater attention." (*GK* 317) Chinese classics — the "Four Books" or Confucian teachings, is "A REAL book". However, the value of Chinese classics is not recognized by all men, but knowledge in it could be gained by all men. Pound warned persons who knew nothing about Confucianism: "When one knows enough one can find wisdom in the Four Classics. When one does not know enough one's eye passes over the page without seeing it." (*GK* 17) "A man acquires knowledge in order that he may be a more complete man, a finer individual, a fuller, more able, more interesting companion for other men." (*SP* 191)

3.3 Becoming a Man with *Ren* 仁

To acquire knowledge is by no means an effortless process. "Real knowledge", Pound wrote in *Guide to Kulchur*, "does NOT fall off the page into one's stomach." (*GK* 107) Practicing only meditation does not produce results. Pound recorded Kung's regret on the opening pages of *Guide to Kulchur*:

> Said Kung the Master: I have passed whole days without food, entire nights without sleep for the sake of my meditation, and in this there was no real use. It wd. have been better to have studied something in particular.
>
> 知
>
> 人 (*GK* 19)

Confucius complained that he devoted his sleep and energy to meditation but only found it fruitless. Knowledge itself came not from introspection but from objective observation. To achieve knowledge, one needed *xue* 学 (studying). This was repeatedly emphasized by Pound. In "Digest of the analects", Pound ended the essay with his pictographical explanation of *xue* 学:

> The dominant element in the sign for learning in the love of learning chapter is a mortar. That is, the knowledge must be ground into fine powder.
>
> 學 (*GK* 21)

The importance of learning was advocated by Pound in his discussion of *The Analects*. "Learning" meant not only to gain knowledge through reading books or listening to others, but also to obtain knowledge through practice, and Pound's concept of learning puts emphasis on the latter. Of course, his interpretation of the Chinese character 学 was based on his pictographically reading of the word. It probably seemed ridiculous for some serious sinologists to interpret *xue* 学 in such an incredible way, but such an unbelievable interpretation reflected Pound's awareness of the essence of Confucian learning — learning through practice. "The knowledge must be ground into fine powder" emphasized that knowledge must be learned in life through practice like the wheat being ground into powder. The process of learning stood an important step in Confucian self-cultivation. Pound wrote in *Zhong Yong*: "Love of study is near to knowledge." (*Con* 153-155)

Pound put emphasis on the importance of learning and the pleasure of study in *The Cantos*: "To study with the white wings of time passing / is not that our delight[?]" (Canto LXXIV 457) The original version of these lines stands at the very beginning of *The Analects*: "*xue er shi xi zhi bu yi yue hu* 学而时习之不亦乐乎?" Pound's inventive version "the white wings of time passing", resulted from his ideogrammic reading of 时 and 习 (Kenner, 1971: 475). The rendering suffered from violent criticism whenever Pound's Confucian translations were under discussion. But few critics noticed that Pound varied his translation in *The Analects*.

> Study with the season winging past, is not this pleasant? (*Con* 195)

The variation might show that Pound didn't abusively interpret Chinese characters. He meticulously and pensively chose proper words to create a sort of poetic beauty hidden between the lines of *The Cantos*. "The white wings of time passing" expressed exactly the scene of "the seasons winging past" when a man was immersed in study. The image "white wings" permeated power and energy moving in a vast space, and the man who was studying was another image that was relatively stable in the space, which drew a wonderful philosophic picture.

Pound argued: "To know is to act knowledge." (*Con* 199-200) Cheadle (1997: 95) contended: "Self-discipline…is not really enough… There must be consequent action." The "consequent action" is based on self-knowledge: "Shun in knowing himself he was a sage and he acted on the clarity of his self-knowledge." (*Con* 133)

Expanding knowledge was what Pound pursued for his lifetime and the curious want of self-knowledge persisted in his tireless reading and writing in response to what the society needed. Pound attached importance to the knowledge that "to improve their curiosity and not to fake, though that is not enough" was the answer Pound gave to "the young" in an interview in 1960 (Cheadle, 1997: 69). "Curiosity" or the "completion of the cognitions", Cheadle (1997: 69) discussed, is only a beginning. The Confucian *Tao* (or *Dao* 道, Pound's "process") begins with knowledge and proceeds to verbal precision, to self-discipline, then to the order in the family, to the state, and ultimately to the "empire" or world as a whole.

The goal of self-cultivation is to cultivate and perfect oneself to be a profound man, a "real man" and "manhood" in Pound's term and a man possessing *ren* 仁 (*ren zhe* 仁者, or *jun zi* 君子). "Hence the man who keeps a rein on himself (君子) looks straight into his own heart at the things wherewith there is no trifling." "Hence the man of true breed looks straight into his heart even when he is alone." (*Con* 101) *Ren zhe* or *jun zi* at the highest state is a sage, such as Yao, Shun, Yu and King Wen in Chinese history. This idea of cultivating abilities to live through introspection informs a self-revealing moment in *The Cantos*:

> J'ai eu pitié des autres.
> Pas assez! Pas assez!
> For me nothing. But that the child
> walk in peace in her basilica,
> The light there almost solid.
> 力 li^4
> 行 hsing^2
> 近 chin^4
> 乎 hu^1 2154
> 仁 jên^2
> holding that energy is near to benevolence. (Canto XCIII 648-649)

The first two lines in French are translated as "I have had compassion for others. Not enough! Not enough!" "The child" in the next line refers to Pound's beloved daughter Mary who wrote a poem in Italian which contained the sentiment "for me nothing, stillness-stillness outlasting all wars". Pound remembered that "her most vividly during her years at Gais and at moments in Rapallo during WWII". "The light" is one of Pound's favorite images in his later cantos. The whole line reads: "Divinity manifested in natural intelligence...flowing."[①] The five characters correspond to the line "holding that energy is near to benevolence", which is from *Zhong Yong* 中庸 focusing on how to achieve *ren* 仁. As a father, his deep and strong love toward his daughter Mary is also highlighted in the lines. Love your family and love people beyond the family. One never has enough compassion for others, and it's never enough to love others. Only when a man uses enough "energy" can he get close to *ren* 仁 and hence enjoy the love of light. Pound reiterated the light in Canto XCV:

> That the crystal wave mount to flood surge
> 近 chin4
> 乎 hu1
> 仁 jên2
> The light there almost solid. (Canto XCV 664).

In Pound's earthly paradise, the universal love of light is indispensable.

That "humanity is to love men" is Pound's translation of *ren zhe ai ren* 仁者爱人. Pound used six Chinese characters to stress the importance of Confucian love:

> 仁 為 親
> 親 寶 以 (Canto XCVII 696)

The original text for this quotation is *ren qin yi wei bao* 仁亲以为宝 from *Da Xue*. Pound's translation is that "The lost man [King Wen in exile] does not treasure jewels and such wealth, counting his manhood and the love of his relatives the true treasure." (*Con* 75) Pound put emphasis on love, which linked the self to others. Confucian love is not abstract and it requires the man to love his family members first, spread the love to relatives and friends, and then love men to whom he is socially related. In Confucian ethics, one's love is meaningful only when one shows his love in a way corresponding to his social position. In this sense, Confucian love bonds social members and consolidates the social order.

Pound's belief that a man can become a sage through self-cultivation is based on Mencius's proposition that man is originally good in nature. According to Mencius,

① The interpretations are based on Terrell's *A Companion to the Cantos of Ezra Pound* (1993: 566).

man is inherently born with a good nature which is *si duan* 四端 — *ren* 仁, *yi* 义, *li* 礼, *zhi* 智. Since human nature is innately good, it may seem that it's not necessary to cultivate it. But the problem is that man is liable to do something against his good nature when he is seduced by external forces. In order to resist evil from outside, man needs to develop the four virtues: *ren* 仁, *yi* 义, *li* 礼, *zhi* 智. The four virtues, together with *xin* 信, are called the five constant virtues (*wu chang* 五常), which are a significant Confucian doctrine posed by the prominent Confucian scholar Zhongshu Dong 董仲舒 of the Han Dynasty, and guided the lives of Chinese people for more than 2,000 years. Though Pound did not openly mention this Confucian term in this works, he repeatedly referred to *si duan* in *The Cantos* and quoted *xin* 信 in his prose and poetic writings. He thence valued the five Confucian virtues. What, then, is *xin* 信 in Pound's belief?

Xin 信 was defined by Pound in the 1938 prose work "Mang Tzse" as "the man who stands by his word" (*SP* 85). On the introductory page of his translation of *The Analects*, he wrote the big character 信 occupying half of the page, interpreting it in English as "man standing by his word". Pound's interpretation of the character is consistent in his translations and writings. In the terminology, he defined it as "fidelity to the given word. The man here standing by his word" (*Con* 22). Pound's fondness for this character is a result of his discovery of the meaning of *cheng* 诚 in it. "Man standing by his word" is the man who will not lie to others. If *cheng* lays special emphasis on a kind of internal cognition of self, *xin* then stresses some external presentation of self. A profound person (*ren zhe* 仁者) must possess the virtue of *xin* 信.

To become a wise person needs constant moral development. This moral development, however, can not be accomplished quickly. In other words, self-cultivation is a life-long process requiring constant practice. Pound's idea of a Confucian "steady rise" through self-development is supported by *ri ri xin* 日日新 (day by day make it new), which is Pound's literary and sociopolitical slogan. *Ri ri xin* 日日新 becomes Pound's *xin ri ri xin* 新日日新 in the 1934 essays in the book under the title *Jefferson and/or Mussolini*. In the 1930s, Pound believed that the Confucian doctrine consisted mainly of political renovation or revolution. It did not appear in *The Cantos* until the year of 1938 when the "China Cantos" was published:

Tching prayed on the mountain and
    wrote MAKE IT NEW 新 hsin[1]
on his bath tub
    Day by day make it new 日 jih[4]
cut underbrush,
pile the logs 日 jih[4]
keep it growing.
Died Tching aged years an hundred, 新 hsin[1]
in the 13th of his reign.
    "We are up, Hia is down" (Canto LIII 264-265)

Pound retold the story of Tching (Cheng Tang 成汤) who led the overthrow of the Hia (Xia) Dynasty and founded the Shang Dynasty (1600 BC-1046 BC). The first four lines introduce Tching's idea of renovation, "day by day make it new", and the following three lines show Pound's pictographic reading of the character 新. "Cut" was from the right-hand radical *jin* 斤 from which Pound saw an axe (*fu* 斧) and "pile" was from *li* 立 which means standing. From the lower part of the left-hand radical, Pound found *mu* 木 which means log or tree. So he arrived at the poetic expression "keep it growing". Pound's interpretation might be unreasonable for some somber sinologists; however, his inventive reading conveyed the connotation of *xin* 新 by using the three verbs "cut", "pile" and "keep", because renovation or revolution needed power, energy and even violence. *Xin ri ri xin* 新日日新 in this poem reveals Pound's sociopolitical orientation.

After World War II, especially after *The Pisan Cantos*, Pound shifted from political concerns to self-cultivation because he found "a man's paradise is his good nature" (Canto XCIII 643). To put it succinctly, Pound concluded that an empire order couldn't establish an earthly paradise and that paradise was built by a man with "good nature" and constant renovation. He translated *xin* 新 in *The Great Digest*:

In letters of gold on T'ang's bathtub:
    AS THE SUN MAKES IT NEW
    DAY BY DAY MAKE IT NEW
    YET AGAIN MAKE IT NEW.

> It is said in the K'ang Proclamation:
> *He is risen, renewing the people.* (*Con* 36)

"*Renewing the people*" in italics, indicates Pound's special concern for it, and "renew the people" is reiterated by Pound shortly in his note under these passages (*Con* 39). An earthly paradise depends on renovation or self-cultivation. Since the first appearance of "新日日新" in Canto LIII, the characters "日新" or "新" repeatedly appear in the later cantos (Canto LIV 278; Canto LXXXVIII 591; Canto XCIII 649; Canto XCIV 662; Canto XCVII 695; Canto XCVIII 704; Canto CX 800). *Ri ri xin* 日日新 "remained central to him throughout his career" (Cheadle, 1997: 37). "Indeed, it is not the idealized state of being perfect but the result of concrete steps by which one becomes constantly renewed and invigorated toward a higher horizon of perfection that motivates the Confucian to forge ahead in the task of self-realization." (Tu, 1984: 387) "新日日新", literally speaking, is "renew, day day renew". Pound informed his readers in the introductory page of *The Analects*: "What the reader can find here is a set of measures whereby, at the end of a day, to learn whether the day has been worth living." (*Con* 194)

Learning for oneself or learning for the sake of one's self (*wei ji zhi xue* 为己之学) defines what Confucianism is. It derives from Confucius's famous deploring of the inappropriate purpose of learning: *gu zhi xue zhe wei ji, jin zhi xue zhe wei ren* 古之学者为己，今之学者为人" (*Lun Yu* XIV. 25). Pound rendered it as follows: "In the old days men studied to make themselves, now they study to impress others." (*Con* 259) Confucianism centered on self-cultivation which was what Pound found to be the fundamental difference between Confucianism and Christianity. He fully understood the importance of self-cultivation and wrote in *Confucius*: "From the Emperor, Son of Heaven, down to the common man, singly and all together, this self-discipline is the root." (*Con* 33) Only when the root is firmly planted can branches grow prosperously. Pound said:

> …having attained self-discipline, they set their own houses in order; having order in their own homes, they brought good government to their own states; and when their states were well governed, the empire was brought into equilibrium. (*Con* 33)

This is Pound's translation of the last three steps of the first chapter of *Da Xue*. If we say this section deals with the first four steps aiming for self-cultivation — fostering personal improvement for moral development, then the next section will focus on the following three steps which are targeted at social development. Pound claimed: "An inner harmony seldom leads to active perturbing of public affairs." (*GK* 225) Self-cultivation is a measure to keep harmony with the universe, which will be fully discussed at the end of this part.

4. Pound's Ethics on Man and Society

Pound embraced Confucianism because he found it focused on "self-discipline and domestic order" (*Con* 57) and stressed the power of domestic order: "One humane family can humanize a whole state." (*Con* 59) The cultivation of self as the center of a relationship represents that the Confucian principle is the continuous development and a holistic approach. Pound believed that "civilization consists in the establishment of a hierarchy of values" (*SP* 90). The Confucian principle, as for Pound, offered a "hierarchy of values" in contrast to Christianity's "mere division between the damned and the saved" (*SP* 90). Thus, what in Confucianism especially attracted him was Confucius's deep concern about humanity and life in this earthly world. Early in *The Cantos*, after an oft-repeated display of "order" in Canto XIII, Pound concluded:

> And Kung gave the words "order"
> and brotherly "deference"
> And said nothing of the "life after death." (Canto XIII 59)

In the 1920s, Pound believed a humane social order would be realized by the practice of "brotherly deference". Pound returned to his thinking on Confucius's philosophical ideas regarding the living and the dead 13 years later in *Guide to Kulchur*: "Nothing cd. be more false than the idea that Kung was preoccupied with the dead. He was concerned with the living." (*GK* 274)

Pound asserted that Confucius's deep concern about the social order made Confucianism superior to any other Western philosophies represented by Aristotle, Christianity and even Odysseus:

> The sense of responsibility, the need for coordination of individuals expressed in Kung's teaching differs radically from early Christian absolutism and from the maritime adventure morals of Odysseus or the loose talk of argumentative greeks. (*GK* 38)

In comparison, "there is no sense of social order in the teaching of the irresponsible protagonist of the New Testament," Pound deplored (*GK* 38). "The decline of Christian ethics" (*SP* 61) compelled Pound to solicit help from Eastern philosophy.

Pound was critical of Western philosophy which "is utterly irresponsible…and is at no point impregnated with a feeling for the whole people" (*GK* 29). In contrast, Confucianism encourages men "to know men" and "to love men" (*GK* 18) and Confucius's thought "is never something scaled off the surface of facts. It is root volition branching out, the ethical weight is present in every phrase" (*GK* 279). To put it simply, Confucius is "filled with a sense of responsibility. He and his interlocutors live in a responsible world, they think for the whole social order" (*GK* 29).

4.1 Establishing the Order in the Family — *Xiao Ti* 孝悌

For an illustration of the relationship between the individual and the state, more attention should be given to *The Great Digest*. Pound recognized the essential characteristics of *The Great Digest* when he first translated it in 1928 and still considered it essential 20 years later in an essay he wrote in Italy. Tim Redman argued:

> During the period of the late 1930s and particularly during the Second World War, Pound became convinced that the philosophy of Confucius, along with economic reform, offered the best hope for an enduring and just social order, and he worked to translate Confucius into Italian and publish his work in Italy. (Redman, 1999: 258)

Actually, Pound retranslated *Da Xue* into Italian in 1941-1942 (a new Italian translation of *Zhong Yong* was published in 1945). *The Great Digest* offers eight steps to realize an orderly and harmonious society. The first four steps (the investigation of things, the acquisition of knowledge, the sincerity of the will, and the rectification of the heart) aim at realizing self-cultivation which is the root of regulation of the family resulting in the ordering of the nation and lastly the harmony of the world.

Self-cultivation stands in the pivotal place, which bridges the inner world and the outer world. Lan (2005: 106) observed that "in Pound's version of Confucius, as long as one establishes order within oneself or one's family, the resultant benefits will automatically reach society as a whole". From the Poundian-Confucian perspective, self-cultivation paves the way to self-responsibility, and self-responsibility leads to social responsibility. Both self-responsibility and social responsibility are highly significant for Pound's construction of an orderly society. Pound himself had a strong sense of responsibility (Stock, 1961: 173-177).

If we relate self-responsibility to one's responsibility in the family and then social responsibility to what a person should do for the community or the state in which he lives, it seems that we'd better divide people generally into two groups: the ordinary people and the elite, particularly referring to the rulers. Pound insisted that the rulers, compared with the ordinary, ought to take more social responsibilities. It is not like John F. Kennedy's slogan — "my fellow Americans ask not what your country can do for you; ask what you can do for your country"[①]. Actually, it is your right to ask what your country can do for you as you do what you can for your country. Surely, it's impossible to distinguish clearly self-responsibility and social responsibility because the two are interactive and cannot be separated when establishing an orderly society. A man in possession of *ren* 仁 or "a finer man" and "a profound person" must be self-responsible as well as socially responsible. But in the Poundian-Confucian political view, the rulers should take more responsibilities for the just social order. Pound wrote in *Guide to Kulchur*: "The first duty of the state is the maintenance of public order." (*GK* 42) An exploration of Pound's ethics on man and society will start with building the order in the family and then focus on the responsibility in establishing the social order, particularly the rulers' responsibilities.

Since "the government of a state is rooted in keeping order in one's own family", (*Con* 63) then how can the order within the family be established? The word that Pound put the same importance as "order" is "brotherly 'deference'", which can be understood as the Confucian concept *ti* 悌 (Pound also translated it as "brotherliness" or "fraternal affection"). In Confucian ethics, *ti* 悌 is inseparable from *xiao* 孝 (also as *Hsiao*) and they are the premise to establish the order in the family. Pound was fully aware of the importance of *xiao ti* 孝悌 because it ran through his works from the inception of his Confucian study to the comprehensive understanding of Confucianism. In *Guide to Kulchur*, he tentatively interpreted and digested some of Confucius's principles of *The Analects*:

> Duty in the home, deference among all men. Affection among all men and attachment in particular to persons of virtu (or virtue). / Seek friends among equals. / I am pro-Tcheou (in politics) said Koung fu Tseu. / They examined their predecessors. (*GK* 19)

What Pound selected to digest is from *Lun Yu* I. 6, which consists of the general rules

---

① See John F. Kennedy's "Inaugural Address". More information is on http://www.presidency.ucsb.edu/ws/?pid=8032#axzz2jMXWkRbO [2018-12-18].

of another Chinese classic, *Di Zi Gui* 弟子规. It's hard to tell whether Pound read or knew of this book in the year of 1938, but Pound's sharp perception and apprehension could not be ignored because *Di Zi Gui* aims at shaping a person to be a filial son or daughter, a fraternal brother or sister, and eventually to be a responsible social being. Before the Qing Dynasty, it was a compulsory book for the young, and nowadays it has regained the favor of 21st-century parents. As the core principle of Confucianism in making a man, it's necessary to quote Pound's translation and the original Confucian text for comparison:

> Young men should be filial in the home, and *brotherly outside it*; careful of what they say, but once said, stick to it; *be agreeable to everyone*, but develop friendship (further) with the real men; if they have any further energy left over, let them devote it to culture.[①] (*Con* 195)
>
> *Di zi ru ze xiao, chu ze ti, jin er xin, fan ai zhong er qin ren. Xing you yu li, ze yi xue wen.* 弟子入则孝，出则悌，谨而信，泛爱众而亲仁。行有余力，则以学文。(*Lun Yu* I. 6)

Comparing it with the version in *Guide to Kulchur*, the author noticed minor alterations in Pound's interpretation of the *xiao ti* concept. Some of the wordings and sentence patterns may be slightly varied, but the essence of the meaning remains almost the same. Replace "duty" with "be filial" for *xiao* and "deference" with "brotherly" for *ti*, and the rest does not change much. The *xiao ti* concept, like an ethical line, runs through *The Cantos*.

Since "brotherly deference" firstly appeared in Canto XIII, the *xiao ti* concept has been a recurring theme in *The Cantos*, appearing, for example, as "filial fraternal", "filial piety", "filiality", "*Hsiao*" and the ideogram "孝". Pound's poetic expression of the Confucian concept at the beginning of *The Pisan Cantos* indicates that his understanding was almost close to maturity:

> filial, fraternal affection is the root of humaneness
> the root of the process[②] (Canto LXXIV 457)

In Confucian ethics, *xiao* is more important than *ti*, and it is the vital virtue practiced to attain the order within the family. As a baby comes into the world, the first persons

① The italics in this quotation is mine.

② This lines are from *The Analects*: Filiality and brotherliness are the root of manhood, increasing with it [*xiao ti ye zhe, qi wei ren zhi ben yu.* 孝悌也者，其为仁之本与。(*Lun Yu* 1.2)] (*Con* 195)

he comes into contact with inevitably ought to be his parents, and thus his first emotional experiences should be his affection towards his parents (or people who care for him and educate him). The love or affection that a child holds towards his parents is termed *xiao*. *Xiao*, usually translated as "filial piety", is recognized by Pound as "a filiality that binds things together" (Canto XCVIII 706). And "filial piety is very inclusive / it does not include / Family squabbles over / 田 land 钱 money, etcetera / Or pretendings" (Canto XCVIII 711). *Xiao* is the purest and unselfish love that binds the family together and it has nothing to do with "land" and "money". *Xiao* is the primary aspect of *ren* 仁, which is, as discussed before, "to love men". Therefore, the practice of *xiao*, the earliest and basic expression of love, is one of the requisites for the realization of *ren* 仁. Pound weighed the value of *xiao* as a way to attain *ren* 仁 later:

> 敬 reverence
>
> and τὸ χαλόν
>
> order 孝
>
> "Parents naturally hope their sons will be gentlemen." (Canto XCVIII 711)

Pound defined *jing* 敬 in two ways: One was fraternal reverence; the other extended reverence from the human world to the world of nature, which will be discussed later. In this context, *jing* 敬 is "reverence", a kind of respect towards parents in a narrow sense and a sort of respect to any people who are worthy of being respected in a broad sense. The Greek phrase "τὸ χαλόν" that means beauty and the English word "order" are set between "敬" and "孝". Pound realized that the orders both in families and in the state couldn't be separated from the performing of *xiao* 孝 and *jing* 敬. Pound used the Greek phrase "beauty" to celebrate the Confucian order and the practice of *xiao* and *jing*. "Parents" widely recognize the truth that *xiao* is the basic step for "their sons" to "be gentlemen". The English word "order" and the Chinese character "孝", standing side by side in the same line, echo with Kung's words "order" and "brotherly 'deference'" listed in Canto XIII.

Ti 悌 is another important virtue of achieving the external order for Pound, although it couldn't share equal importance with *xiao* 孝 in the Confucian system. Tay (1977: 114) explained: "Fraternal affection or 悌 *t'i* is only a supplementary concept since one who truly practices *xiao* will inevitably be kind to his brothers and sisters, otherwise the parents' feeling may be violated." This explanation is in accordance with the traditional and narrow understanding of this Confucian concept. Traditionally, *ti* 悌 means that the younger family member respects his elder siblings in the family. A typical example is *Kong Rong rang li* 孔融让梨, a real historical story about the four-year-old Kong Rong (153–208, a litterateur of the Han Dynasty) who chose the smallest pear so as to leave bigger ones for his elder brothers and younger brothers. This is a narrow-sense understanding of this virtue. In a broader sense, it encourages the younger family members to show respect for all elder persons no matter whether they are from the family or not. Confucius said *si hai zhi nei jie xiong di ye* 四海之内皆兄弟也, and Pound translated this as "all men within the four seas are elder and younger brothers" (*Con* 244). Pound's interpretation coincided with the broad-sense of *ti*. All men in the world live in one big family and all are sisters and brothers. Therefore, the principle of *ti* operates as a social contract coordinating all individual activities so as to maintain the functionality of society as a whole.

In this sense, Pound's interpretation of the concept *ti* is in accordance with his understanding of *ren* 仁 which Pound wrote "humanity, (is) to love men" (*ren zhe ai ren* 仁者爱人). Thinking back to "出则悌", the author found that Pound's "deference among all men" and "brotherly outside it (the home)" deliver the same meaning — love men. Considering Pound's translation of *fan ai zhong* 泛爱众 in the same Confucian principle into "be agreeable to everyone", it provides more evidence of Pound's preference for "brotherly deference" abroad over "brotherliness" at home.① Actually, "deference among all men", "brotherly outside it (the home)" or "be agreeable to everyone" is a child's love extended from parents to non-family members. This love and its extension capture the key point of *ren* 仁, namely Pound's "humanity" (to love men). To highlight the importance of *ren* in establishing and maintaining the social order, Pound wrote: "Beyond the civic order, / L'AMOR." (Canto XCIV 654) L'AMOR means "love" and the "civic order" makes the lines into a Confucian concept. (Terrell, 1993: 572) Pound reiterated the significance of love in "A Visiting Card" in this way:

```
R O M A
O     M
M     O
A M O R
```
(*SP* 327)

① Legge's (2009: 140) exegeses 入出 "coming in, going out" means "at home" and "abroad", respectively.

Pound made a square with four letters A, M, O and R, creating an intriguing crossword puzzle effect. The vertices of a diagonal line (bottom left, top right) are the letter A, while those of another diagonal line (top left, bottom right) are the letter R. If one reads the words beginning with A on the four sides of the square, it must be "AMOR" no matter from which direction (vertically or laterally) he reads. "Amor" is the Latin name of the Roman god of love — Cupid. Interestingly enough, if one reads the words beginning with R on the four sides of the square, it must be "ROMA" no matter from which direction (vertically or laterally) he reads. "Roma" is the Italian name for "Rome". Pound overtly lauded Roman love. Perhaps the square can help to answer why Pound has "chosen a priest rather than one of the two Protestant ministers" at DTC near Pisa. "… a Confucianist and a Catholic… get along very well." (Flory, 2003: 147) The love starting from two vertices makes a seemingly sealed space that will extend infinitely. Love or L'AMOR, as an eternal life force, is the core of Confucian humanism. *Ren* 仁, a central concept of Confucianism, now becomes a foundation of a harmonious society.

Since *xiao* was the basis of becoming a "gentleman" (*ren zhe* 仁者) and *ti* manifested a universal love towards "everyone", Pound wrote the line: "Filial, fraternal affection is the root of humaneness." (Canto LXXIV 457) *Xiao ti* 孝悌 is not only the root of *ren* 仁 but also "the root of the process" [*Dao* 道]. Tay argued: "If the ultimate perfection and goal of *tao* 道 is the attainment and preservation of order from personal and familial levels to the national one, *hsiao* is indeed the basis, for as a moral virtue it guides the individual's behavior in the family, thus involving two primary levels of order." (Tay, 1977: 115) From this practical viewpoint, to understand the function of *xiao* as a way to reach *Dao* was convincing, but obviously ignores Pound's emphasis on *ti*.

Pound's tireless investigation and interest in Confucianism, if considered from a practical point of view, are to establish a harmonious existence of man with man, and man with society in the West. According to the above discussion, filial piety and "brotherly deference" are as important as "order" because *xiao* leads to a sound familial order and *ti* helps to develop a harmonious society. For Pound, in his late years of Confucian study, he believed that *xiao* rather than *ti* formed the basis because the family was a place where one's communication started. That's why Pound gave more thoughts and poetic space to *xiao* in his later cantos. As a matter of fact, Pound's understanding of *ti* 悌 is consistent and persistent since the beginning of his Confucian study; however, his comprehension of *xiao* 孝 is not static but dynamic although his awareness of the importance of *xiao* is comparatively late. *Xiao*, interpreted from "duty" to "filial" and lastly to a direct citation of the Chinese character "孝" in "Thrones", indicates Pound's increasing understanding and focus on this Confucian virtue. Besides the various forms of *xiao* appearing in his works, a specific example may be found at the beginning of *The Pisan Cantos*:

> Yaou chose Shun to longevity
> who seized the extremities and the opposites
> holding true course between them
> shielding men from their errors
> cleaving to the good they had found
> holding empire as if not in a mortar with it
> nor dazzled thereby
> wd / have put the old man, *son père* on his shoulders
> and gone off to some barren seacoast (Canto LXXIV 462)

The last two lines are Mencius's answer to a hypothetical question raised by his student Tao Ying 桃应. It is said that Shun 舜 was a devotedly filial son and a fraternal brother and hence Yao 尧 (Pound's Yaou) gave the crown to Shun as a reward for Shun's filial piety. Pound's poetic expression was that "Yaou chose Shun to longevity". The hypothesis goes like this: "When Shun was Emperor and Kao Yao (Gao Tao 皋陶) was the judge, if Shun's father killed a man, what was to be done?" Mencius responded that nothing could be done but to apprehend him. In this case, Shun had no choice but to follow the decision of the judge, which represented the law of the state. But as a filial son, he would have a strong sense of guilt to leave his father alone and hence Mencius's answer went as follows:

> Shun looked upon casting aside the Empire as no more than discarding a worn shoe. He would have secretly carried the old man (Shun's father [*son père*]) on his back and fled to the edge of the Sea and lived there happily, never giving a thought to [ruling] the Empire. (*Mencius*, VIIA: 153)

This expresses without any doubt that filiality is the root of manhood.

Mencius's case was far more complicated since Shun was an emperor as well as a law-maker. On the one hand, as a law-maker, he had a duty to enforce the law; on the other hand, as a dutiful son, he had a responsibility to protect his old father. Shun's decision and actions are proper for fulfilling his duties as a ruler and a son. The fact that Shun was not lost in such a dilemma proved that he was a well self-cultivated man and his choice permitted him not to break the order which had been established under his leadership, and also allowed him to continue to be a filial son. Such a decision reflects the principle of *zhong* 中 (Pound's chung), which is a positive standard of evaluation in Confucian thinking.

In this stanza, Pound apparently related Shun's hypothetical behavior with the principle of *zhong* 中. Pound described Shun with the quotations from *Zhong Yong* 中庸: "seized the extremities and the opposite", "holding true course between them" and "holding empire as if not in a mortar with it". *Zhong*, one of the most important Confucian doctrines, aroused Pound's attention in the early years of his Confucian study. Looking back to Canto XIII, we can see Pound's early interest in this doctrine:

> And he said
> "Anyone can run to excesses,
> It is easy to shoot past the mark,
> It is hard to stand firm in the middle."
>
> And they said: If a man commit murder
> Should his father protect him, and hide him?
> And Kung said:
> He should hide him. (Canto XIII 59)

In the first Confucian canto, Pound has a clear recognition of *zhong* — "stand firm in the middle". The first four lines of this excerpt center on the idea of *zhong* which is Pound's preliminary but pertinent understanding of the term; the last four lines, interestingly enough, follow Pound's exaggeration of a Confucius's anecdote about father and son, which is similar to Shun's hypothetical situation. In *Lun Yu* XIII. 18, Confucius once argued with Ye Gong 叶公 about what "honest characters" were. Pound's version of the anecdote reads:

> The Duke of Sheh said to Kung-tze: There are honest characters in my village, if a man steals a sheep his son will bear witness to it. Kung-tze said: There are honest men in my village with this difference; a father will conceal his son's doing, and a son his father's. There's honesty (straight seeing) in that, too. (*Con* 251)

In Canto XIII, Pound elevated the crime from theft to murder and hence the description about Shun in Canto LXXIV echoed with his writing about *zhong* and honesty in Canto XIII.

Zhong 中, the idea of the "middle course", is what Pound spoke highly of. *Zhong* does not mean a compromising attitude in the practice of moral principles. A person with personal order must "stand firm in the middle" like an unwobbling pivot in his moral decision, but he makes decisions according to actual situations. His decisions or specific actions must meet the judgment on the relevance of the moral standard which is *yi* 义 (righteousness). Actually, *The Pisan Canto* ends with *zhong* 中 (Pound's chung): "John Adams, the Brothers Adam / there is our norm of spirit / our 中 chung / whereto we pay our homage." (Canto LXXXIV 560) As for Pound, *zhong* is the norm of spirit, to which we should pay our homage.

4.2 Establishing Social Orders — *Li*, *Yi* 礼, 义

"Put order in the home in order to govern the country." (*Con* 65) A just social order, which is the ultimate purpose of self-discipline, ought to be under discussion after building a sound familial order by practicing the *xiao ti* virtue. Theoretically, once the personal order and the familial order are set up, the social order will be automatically realized; practically, everyone is responsible for establishing the social order. But Pound required the rulers to take more responsibilities than the common men for social harmony. Pound started his pondering on the social order as he considered what the government or the state could possibly do for the people. "'Ch'ing Ming' is the first step toward conditioning the government to do its work," Pound contended, "Government's job is to feed the people, that is its FIRST job." (*SP* 94). "The first duty of the state is the maintenance of public order." (*GK* 42) Food and order are dependent but interrelated. Food and order are metaphorically compared by Pound to "bread and circuses": "If imperial thought runs to keeping that order free from inruption and disturbance jammed into it from without, the feeding problem at some point arises." (*GK* 42) The importance of food is reiterated in "Thrones": "Food is the root. / Feed the people." (Canto XCIX 715) Therefore, defining the job and duty of the government is found in the Confucian doctrine of *zheng ming* 正名 (Pound's Ch'ing Ming or Cheng Ming), which is a key term in Pound's Confucianism.

Zheng ming 正名 is an emblem of Pound's Confucianism and reflects his concern about verbal precision for most Poundian scholars and readers of *The Cantos*. Pound's 正名 in the literary field, named by Lan (2005: 46, 55) as "linguistic precision" or "poetic precision", is significant for Pound's theory of poetry. A cluster of Confucian terms, such as *cheng* 诚, *xin* 信 and *zhong* 忠, are important for the lesson of precise verbal definition and verbal fidelity. Lan had an elaborate explanation and analysis in "Confucianism and Pound's rethinking of language", which occupies a quarter of his book *Ezra Pound and Confucianism — Remaking Humanism in the Face of Modernity*. He (Lan, 2005: 46) argued: "The two Confucian doctrines of *zheng ming* 正名 and *cheng yi* 诚意 are crucial to Pound's formulation of a new theory of language... At the core of Pound's new theory of language is a belief that Poetry...represents the highest degree of linguistic precision." This study is meaningful because Pound confirmed: "The art of not being exploited begins with 'Ch'ing Ming'!" (*GK* 244) But Pound's 正名 contains many more meanings than "word and thing". What centers on, here, are "name and function" (Cheadle, 1997: 257) — the political and ethical meaning of 正名 in Pound's Confucianism.

The appeal of *zheng ming* appears on the second page of "Digest of *The Analects*" in *Guide to Kulchur* (1938). Pound's sharp perception impressed the author again for he grasped this fundamental doctrine of Confucianism even though "正名" was not a term in *Da Xue* and *Zhong Yong* but only occurred once in *The Analects*. It's hard to determine the exact time when Pound began to connect with or study this term, but the *zheng ming* passage was included in Pound's first selection of "Digest". Moreover, its first occurrence in *The Cantos* is at the end of Canto LI (1937), in almost the same period as *Guide to Kulchur*. After that, it became a recurring theme in *The Cantos* so that Cheadle (1997: 9) remarked that "this last phase of his Confucianism is marked by a return to what he regarded as Confucian fundamentals, with a concern for precise verbal definitions at the center of them all". Pound's complete comprehension of this doctrine lies in his thoughtful rendering of the *zheng ming* passage in his 1950 translation of *Lun Yu*:

> 1. Tse-lu said: The lord of Wei is waiting for you to form a government, what are you going to do first?
>
> 2. He [Confucius] said: Settle the names (determine a precise terminology).
>
> 3. Tse-lu said: How's this, you're divagating, why fix'em?
>
> 4. He said: You bumpkin! Sprout! When a proper man do(es)n't know a thing, he shows some reserve.
>
> 5. If words (terminology) are not (is not) precise, they cannot be followed out, or completed in action according to specifications.
>
> 6. When the services (actions) are not brought to true focus, the ceremonies and music will not prosper; where rites and music do not flourish punishments will be misapplied, not make bullseye, and the people won't know how to move hand or foot (what to lay hand on,

or stand on).

7. Therefore the proper man must have terms that can be spoken, and when uttered be carried into effect; the proper man's words must cohere to things, correspond to them (exactly) and no more fuss about it. (*Con* 249)

Hardly can readers without Confucian knowledge understand the intricate meaning of the doctrine only by reading Pound's translation or Legge's "to rectify the names of all things". Historical and political contexts should be considered.

The *zheng ming* concept comes from *The Analects* XIII. 3. It is reported that the disciple Zi Lu 子路 asked Confucius what he was going to do first if the Lord of Wei (卫国) invited him to head the state. "*Zheng ming*," Confucius replied briefly and clearly. On hearing the answer, Zi Lu was puzzled. Confucius explained that if *ming* was not correct, language could not make sense; as a consequence, laws and rites would not be followed, leading to the collapse of society. Confucius's notion of *zheng ming* actually looks ambiguous. An authentic interpretation of the doctrine is from Zhu Xi 朱熹 whose explanation is based on Sima Qian's① record of a historical context for the conversation about *zheng ming* between Zi Lu and Confucius.

In order to fully comprehend the *zheng ming* concept, it is necessary to recall the historical context. At the time of the conversation between Zi Lu and Confucius, the sage was residing in the state of Wei where Zhe (辄), the young ruler of the state, was in danger of losing his throne to his self-exiled father, Kuai Kui (蒯聩), who fled Wei after a failed plot against Duke Ling's (卫灵公, Kuai Kui's father) young wife, Nan zi (南子). Four years after Kuai Kui's exile, Duke Ling died and left the kingdom to his grandson Duke Zhe, Kuai Kui's son. Since the father was still alive, Duke Zhe's throne was questioned and, at the same time, Kuai Kui was supported by some powerful lords of the state attempting to fight for the dukedom. It was in this historical background that Duke Zhe solicited help from Confucius. Confucius's reply indicates that Duke Zhe should follow the duty and obligation of a son and abdicate the crown to his exiled father. It was in this historical context that Zhu Xi, in his commentary on the *zheng ming* passage, specified *ming* as the names of father and son. He explained: "At that time Zhe did not treat his father as father, … and thus the relationship between names and the substance of names was disrupted. That is why Confucius held

① Sima Qian (145? BC-86? BC) is a Chinese historian of the early Han Dynasty (206 BC-AD 220), known as the father of Chinese historiography for his *Records of the Grand Historian* (*Shi Ji* 史记). The history covers more than 2,000 years from the Yellow Emperor to his time, during the reign of Emepror Wu of Han.

the rectification of names as the foremost thing to accomplish." (Lan, 2005: 47) To put it simply, *zheng ming* stipulates the foundational codes of feudal social relations, such as the relationship between father and son, or ruler and subject. Zhu Xi's commentary was influential for centuries, and hence there is no reason to doubt that it also influenced Pound.

Zheng ming, realized in practical life, is *li* 礼 (propriety or the rites). *Li* 礼, as one of *si duan*, is a way to practice 内圣外王. Confucius loved the rites, in *The Analects* III. 17, when Zi Gong (子贡, Pound's Tze-Kung or Ts'ze) "wanted to eliminate the sheep from the sacrifice to the new moon," the sage refuted, "You, Ts'ze, love the sheep, I love the rite." (*Con* 203) Although the ideogram "礼" never singly appeared in Pound's works, it didn't necessarily mean that he ignored the importance of "礼". The left part of "礼" is "礻" (示). In the terminology section, "示" was the first item listed, and Pound defined it as "the light descending (from the sun, moon, and stars). To be watched as a component in ideograms indicating spirits, rites, ceremony" (*Con* 20). Pound's interpretation of *li* is mainly manifested in his translation of *The Analects* in which Pound emphasized the social dimensions of the word. Cheadle (1997: 133) discussed that a man who has "good manner, social grace, a sense of etiquette" can practice *li* 礼. Pound's translation of *li* is frequently "ceremony", "ceremonial" or "rites", occasionally "precise observance" (*Con* 197) or "etiquette" (*Con* 203). Good manners are a way to produce peace. Pound wrote in Canto XCIX:

> Peace comes of good manners
> feng^{1} su$^{2\text{-}5}$ li feng su
> INTENZIONE li feng su jang^{4} (Canto XCIX 718)

Good manners become *feng*^{1} *su*$^{2\text{-}5}$ (风俗 in Chinese characters). The importance was made in the fact that *feng su* was written twice by Pound in such a limited space.

Rarely did Pound use either the ideogram "礼" or the Chinese letter *li* in his prose and poetry, but some reference to *li* explicitly contained the meaning of propriety and the Confucian codes of ethics. One of the most important Confucian social norms and ethical codes is expressed in this poetic form:

> that the king 王 shd / be king
> 王 (Canto XCIV 661)

王王 (*wang wang*), invented by Pound, appeared not for once in *The Cantos*. In Canto LXXXIX, Pound stated:

> Name for name, king for king
> 王 wang
> 王 wang (Canto LXXXIX 611)

Wang wang 王王 (king for king) derives from the Confucian principle of "君君 臣臣 父父 子子" meaning that a king should be a king, a minister should be a minister, a father should be a father, and a son should be a son. And the root of this idea is *zheng ming* 正名. Everyone should do what is right or what is fit for his position: "The prince uses his ministers according to the prescribed ceremonial, ministers serve the prince by their sincerity." (*Con* 204) The ethical implication of the Confucian social norm "君君 臣臣 父父 子子" is interpreted below:

> The surname, and the 9 arts.
> The father's word is compassion;
> The son's, filiality.
> The brother's word: mutuality;
> The younger's word: deference.
> Small birds sing in chorus,
> Harmony is in the proportion of branches
> as clarity (chao[1]).
> Compassion, tree's root and water-spring;
> The state: order, inside a boundary;
> Law: reciprocity. (Canto XCIX 728)

Based on the Confucian ethical doctrine "君君 臣臣 父父 子子", the phrase *king king* 王王 invented by Pound indicates his higher requirement for rulers, especially the head of the state. The principle that a king should conduct himself as a king showed Pound's special expectation for the head of the state. Pound analyzed the relationship of the state and the individuals, and criticized the lack of good rulers in England:

> The state exists for the individual, but in our time the individual who does not deem his own acts and thought in certain ways and degrees up and down as to their use to the state (that is the universitas, the congeries of humans grouped in the state) is an inferior

individual.

The lack of such a scale and ambition, ends up in the gang now ruling England. The "best of England" having gone out and got shot in the first months of the 1914 war. (*GK* 190)

Therefore, the lack of self-discipline and self-knowledge "ends up in the gang now ruling England".

Pound believed that "one man can bring the state to an orderly course" (*Con* 61). Pound once proclaimed that "for 2,500 years whenever there has been order in China or in any part of China, you can look for a Confucian at the root of it" (*J/M* 113). "A Confucian" is developed into *yi ren* 一人 (one man, Pound's *i jin*), which becomes a recurring motif in his later cantos. The direct reason for the phrase comes from a meeting at St. Elizabeths Hospital with a Confucian scholar, Carson Chang (张君劢, 1886-1969).① Pound said to him that four Confucians working together could save China. Chang replied: "Four? *One* is enough." (Terrell, 1993: 581) Then "one Confucian" must be a man who is righteous, in accord with propriety and in possession of *ren* 仁. Obviously, a self-disciplined ruler grounded in self-knowledge is the basis of a good Confucian government. Actually, a good reflection of the ruler's personal order is the social-political order, which is emphasized in *The Analects* repeatedly: "Disciplines himself and brings tranquility to the hundred clans." (*Con* 262) Pound put down four Chinese characters vertically in *Guide to Kulchur*:

一
言
偾
事

OR ONE WORD WILL RUIN IT ALL (*GK* 357)

The complete version is *yi yan fen shi, yi ren ding guo* 一言偾事，一人定国 from *Da Xue* (大学) which means "one word will ruin the business, and one man can bring the state to an orderly course" (*Con* 61).

① Carson Chang (Junmai Zhang 张君劢, 1886-1969) is a representative figure of the second generation of Contemporary New Confucianism. In 1958, Junmai Zhang, with the other three important figures Junyi Tang 唐君毅, Zongsan Mou 牟宗三 and Fuguan Xu 徐复观 published "A manifesto on Chinese culture to the world". This work is often referred to as the "New Confucian Manifesto", although that phrase never occurs in it.

The idea of "depending on one man" is a flourishing topic in Pound's later cantos and the Chinese characters 一人 appear four times (Canto LXXXVI 583; Canto LXXXIX 620; Canto XCIV 659; Canto XCV 664). The first time it appears gives us a glimpse into Pound's own uncertainty regarding his belief in the idea:

> 貌 mao[4]
> 亦
> 尚
> 一
> 人
> It may depend on one man
> …as in the case of Edwardus (Canto LXXXVI 583)

The five ideograms in vertical add no more meaning to the following line "It may depend on one man". In this context, the one who is trustworthy is Edwardus, Edward, Prince of Wales, later Edward VIII and the Duke of Windsor. According to Von Hoesch, a telephone conversation he had had delayed the start of World War II by three years.① It's a pervasive example of what one man can do at a critical moment. Pound repeated his good deed: "And to young Windsor we owe three years' peace" (Canto LXXXIX 621). Several cantos later, Pound wrote:

> YAO's worry: to find a successor
> 一
> 人
> & the three years peace we own Windsor
> '36-'39 (Canto XCV 664-665)

This short excerpt conveys two meanings: It attaches more emphasis on the righteous deed of Edward VIII and the Duke of Windsor, by making the three-year peace concrete — from 1936 to 1939; then, the narration of YAO's "worry" indicates Pound's belief in the importance of one man becomes fixed. YAO 尧, one of the wise emperors in Chinese legend, passed over his own son and named Shun 舜 as his successor. Pound

① Consult Terrell's *A Companion to the Cantos of Ezra Pound* (1993: 484).

mentioned it to reiterate the importance of one man's power in establishing a harmonious state.

The rulers who are righteous and just are the reflection of *yi* 义. Pound praised Kang Xi in "Thrones":

i^{4} 義
Ch'i^{4} 氣
From Kati to Kang Hi 康
two $^{1}/_{2}$s of a seal 熙 (Canto XCVIII 710)

Yi 义, is variously interpreted by Pound as "equity", "equilibrium", "righteous(ness)", "honesty" and "what is right". In Mencius's theory, the virtue of *yi* refers to an innate sense of shame which compels us to do what is right and just. Therefore this term is often rendered as "righteousness" or "justice" in English. In *The Analects*, it is always juxtaposed with *li* 利 (material profits), such as "the proper man understands equity, the small man, profits" (*Con* 207). Pound usually rendered it as "equity" when *yi* appeared as the counterpart of *li*, and *yi* was the solution Pound offered to the problem of usury that had been corrupting the world for years. The ending of *The Great Digest* highlights the opposition which appears in Pound's version:

> That is the meaning of:
> A state does not profit by profits.
> Honesty is the treasure of states. [以义为利也] (*Con* 87-89)

"Honesty is the treasure of states" includes a governmental and economic sense but carries the word into the still broader dimension of ethics. To put it simply, the state or the government should be honest. Pound wrote in the 1938 prose work "Mang Tsze":

> Anyone who mistakes Kung or Mencius for a materialist is a plain unadulterated idiot. Their philosophy is not in the least materialist, it is volitionist.
>
> (1) Arms and defences, (2) food, (3) the faith of the people, if they must be given up, be it in this order. (*SP* 94)

Pound clearly knew that Mencius's economic theory aimed at universal humane benevolence rather than profits. To some degree, for Pound, *yi* 义 equals "the faith of the people" which actually derives from *min wu xin bu li* 民无信不立 [if the people be without faith (fail of their word) nothing stands] (*Con* 245).

Pound must have been deeply impressed by the dialectical relationship between *yi* 义 and *li* 利 because it directly decides whether the state lives or dies. Hence, on the last page of his translation of *Da Xue*, he quoted the last line with both Chinese ideograms and English letters. The pages before and after were deliberately left blank to highlight the significance of the Confucian principle through a visual display using the art of space:

利	EQUITY	國
以	IS	不
義	THE	以
為	TREASURE	利
利	OF	為
也	STATES	(*Con* 91)

The visual display of the words makes its importance impressive and outstanding. Comparing it with the previous translation, namely "honesty is the treasure of states", we naturally draw this conclusion: "Honesty" is "equity". But "honesty" is the people's faith in the government or "the morality of the government" while "'equity' refers to its result"(Tay, 1977: 120). When Pound translated *yi* 义 as "equity", he added more economic significance to this Confucian virtue than what it originally contained. In Pound's view, the importance of economics in the Confucian system was a crucial part in the creation of a humane social order. Truly, economics is a crucial element to keep the social order stable. That's why he blamed Aristotle and said: "Aristotle did not save the world economically" because "Aristotle did not implant a clear concept of money in the general western mind. He saw that money was a measure" (*GK* 190). Perhaps that is the reason why Pound presented Mencius's economic justice as his solution to the problem of usury. What Mencius advocated was two economic systems: the share system and the aid system. Both of them aim not at profits but at benevolence and righteousness.

The ideogram of *yi* 义 or its equivalent English interpretations occurs more than ten times in the late cantos. In Canto LXXXIX, the tension between *yi* 义 and *li* 利 is highlighted by Pound's putting the two characters on the same page. Early in Canto LXXXVII (595), he quoted Mencius's argument with Liang Hui Wang 梁惠王: "Why must say profit." Maybe Pound felt such reminding was still not enough; in Canto LXXXIX, he put the Chinese characters vertically in the English poetic text:

> Levari facias. Louis Philippe suggested that
> Jackson stand firm
> and not sugar his language.
> Public debt was extinguished. 1834.
> 何 ho^{2}
> 必 pi$^{4\text{-}5}$
> 曰 yüeh$^{4\text{-}5}$
> 利 li^{4} (Canto LXXXIX 615)

The quotation is followed by the ironic explanation: "This quotation is not from Mr. Webster." (Canto LXXXIX 616)

Pound also rendered *yi* as "righteous". At the end of Canto LXXVIII, Pound quoted one of Mencius's famous sayings:

> In the spring and autumn
> In "The Spring and Autumn"
> there
> are
> no
> righteous
> wars. (Canto LXXVIII 503)

This is a direct translation of *chun qiu wu yi zhan* 春秋无义战. Pound used the wars in the Spring and Autumn Period to allude to the two world wars which were not righteous. *Yi* 义 is righteousness associated with peace. Pound mentioned it in "Mang Tsze" where he cited Mencius's definition of war as "'leading on the earth to devour men', that is in a prince's wars for more territory" (*SP* 87). In the year of 1938, with his publication of *Guide to Kulchur*, and some pieces of prose like "Mang Tsze", Pound "calls for a return to a Confucian concern for the entire social order. But by the time…the West was heading for another global war" (*GK* 258). At the beginning of "Section: Rock-Drill", the reason for wars is openly denounced by Pound — "lost to all i^{4} 義" (Canto LXXXVI 583). Wars are ways for governments to gain profits. There is no holy reason for a government to launch a war. Without a proper or righteous reason, the wars cannot last long. In Canto LXXXIX, Pound stated:

> Government wanted "of deposit, not circulation".
>
> 義 i^4
>
> Without historic black-out
>
> they cannot maintain perpetual wars. (Canto LXXXIX 614-615)

The relationship between *yi* and *li* is explained by the Master in this way: "The superior man in everything considers righteousness to be essential. He performs it according to the rules of propriety. He brings it forth in humility. He completes it with sincerity." (Tay, 1977: 49) Rules of propriety should always be the concrete manifestation of righteousness, and in turn, righteousness is preserved by observing propriety. As to the formalities of propriety, the Master considers it as less significant. Rules of propriety may change, but the principle of righteousness must be strictly adhered to (Tay, 1977: 50). Simply speaking, *li* 礼 as a social code is supposed to change with passing time and be varied across different places. For instance, "when Pound and Dr. Chang (Carsun Chang 张君劢) took their leave of each other, Pound bowed to Dr. Chang over his hands, Chinese-style, and Dr. Chang reciprocated." (*EPCF* 105) However, the essence of propriety or the ability to judge what is right does not change. A person who can always be just and righteous needs to keep in "a state of self-awareness", which is the Confucian virtue *ren*. This self-awareness in action means the realization of righteousness and propriety.

Li 礼, in Pound's view, could not be separated from *yi* 义 and *ren* 仁. In Canto LXXXV (564), he combined *yi* and *li* together — "jen chih i-li / are called chung" instead of listing the virtues in the sequence of Chinese *ren*, *yi*, *li*, *zhi*. Here Pound coined a pattern "i-li" (义-礼), which indicated Pound's awareness of the virtues that were interrelated and interactive. The practical performing of *li* manifests in a man who may be righteous or not, while *yi* ensures a man's right conduct. *Ren*, as discussed above, is the guarantee of the realization of *yi*, but *li* is essential for a person to possess *ren*. Pound translated Zi Lu's (Pound's Tze-yu) quotation of Confucius's words in *The Analects*: "If the gentleman studies the process and loves men, the lower people will study the process and be easy to rule." (*Con* 274) Love for the rites and for men is a way to achieve *ren* 仁. As for *yi* and *li*, *yi* is the inner motive to guide a person to practice *li* in a proper way.

Pound held that the rulers should be responsible for the people, and the responsibility was manifested in "ruling justly". He commented on the function of kingship in "Sparta 776 B.C.": "Kingship, in the domain of matter and energy, is nothing other than the power to amass and distribute." (*GK* 42) This idea also occurs in Pound's "Digest of *The Analects*", the first essay of *Guide to Kulchur*:

> XVI. I. I have heard ever that possessors of kingdoms and the chiefs of great families do not complain of small population, nor of exiguous territory, nor even of the poverty of their peoples, but of the discord between people and ruler. For if each has his part that is due him, there is no pauper, there is harmony, there is no want among the inhabitants. (*GK* 19)

More than a decade later, Pound's version reads: "I have heard that men who have states or head families are not worried about fewness, but worried about fairness [*potter's wheel ideogram: aliter as a verb*: worried about ruling justly]." (*Con* 270)

According to Pound, whether the rulers ruled justly or not depended on the rulers' attitude to *cai* 财 (profits). Pound demonstrated the relationship between *ren* and *cai* by citing a Confucian idea from *Da Xue*: *ren zhe yi cai fa shen, bu ren zhe yi shen fa cai* 仁者以财发身，不仁者以身发财. Pound's own translation in *Confucius* states: "The humane man uses his wealth as a means to distinction, the inhumane becomes a mere harness, an accessory to his takings." (*Con* 83) In the prose section titled "Kung" in *Guide to Kulchur*, Pound let the Chinese characters occupy the whole page to highlight this Confucian idea, and also implicitly lauded Kung as a typical example of *ren zhe* 仁者. In Canto LV, the ideograms were visually displayed:

> If these go to the national treasury
>   they will go out of circulation
> the people thereby deprived,
>   so HIEN-TSONG threw this into commerce
>
> 仁者以財發身不
> 仁者以身發財
>
> (Canto LV 290)

In *Guide to Kulchur*, the Chinese characters occupy all of page 273. Here the Chinese ideograms function as praise for Hien-Tsong (Xian Zong 唐宪宗) who was an emperor during the 9th century in China. Therefore, Pound "did not bother to give advice on how to produce more to a minister whose sole aim was to push up the amount of tribute sweatable from the peasantry" (*GK* 272).

It is neither the first time nor the last time that Pound quoted this Confucian idea to illustrate what a good king should do in regard to his treasury. Early in Canto LII (261), a paraphrase of the same passage occurs: "Good sovereign by distribution / Evil king is known by his imposts." The idea of "good sovereign by distribution" was developed deeper in Canto XCIV (656) in which Pound again inserted the ideograms "梁惠：以財發無以寶" to reiterate "distribution" as an important criterion for judging whether a government is good or not. Here Mencius's advice to Liang Hui Wang 梁惠王 (Pound's King Hwuy of Leang) was used by Apollonius who said to King Vardanes after the latter had shown the former his treasury (Cookson, 2001: 207):

> "This for you, O king, represents wealth, but to me it is mere chaff."
> "How, then," said the other, "and in what manner can I best make use of it?"
> "By spending it," he said, "for you are a king."

The last six Chinese characters mean "by wealth distributed, not by treasure accumulated" (Cookson, 2001: 207). The idea of "spending" is continued in Canto XCIV (675): "TIBERIUS... / by his spending 發." So a good government depends on a wise king who knows how to spend money form his treasury rather than how to accumulate money.

4.3 The Root: *Ben* 本

Pound once proclaimed: "The best government is that which governs least." (Qtd. in Tay, 1977: 53-54) Although the government, in Pound's Confucian view, ought to take more responsibilities than the common men, it does not necessarily mean that the citizens have nothing to contribute to the social order. Pound wrote in Canto XCIX:

> The state is corporate
>   as with pulse in its body

& with Chou rite at the root of it
The root is thru all of it,
a tone in all public teaching:
This is not a work of fiction
nor yet of one man: (Canto XCIX 727-728)

"The state is corporate…not a work of one man" and "Chou rite" is "the root of it". Root, one of Pound's often-used words, is *ben* 本 (Pound's pen) in Chinese. Only when everyone in the state knows what the root is and conducts himself in accord with what it requires will an orderly society be possible. In the last phrase of Pound's Confucianism, Pound attached great importance to *ben ye* 本业 (Pound's pen yeh, root or primary occupation).

Ben 本 derives from Pound's translation of *Da Xue* in which Pound concluded: "This is called knowing the root." (*Con* 47) It follows Tseng's comment — "this is the fourth chapter of the comment giving the gist of the remark (in the Confucian canon) about the root and the branch" (*Con* 47), beside which is attached the ideogram *ben mo* 本末 in large and bold lines. "The root" and "the branch" are Pound's unique and vivid pictographic reading of *ben mo* 本末. According to Pound's pictograph, both of the ideograms evolve from one character *mu* 木 (the tree). If the component "一" lies at the bottom of the tree, it is *ben* 本 (the root); if the component "一" is put above the tree, it is *mo* 末 (the branch). The idea of "root" repeatedly recurs in his Confucian translations and writings. Besides what has been cited in the previous discussions, some valuable "roots" are given below:

Filiality and fraternity are the root,
Talents to be considered as branches. (Canto XCIX 730-731)

The government of the state is rooted in family order. (*Con* 65)

World Order [bringing what is under heaven into equilibrium]
is rooted in the good government of one's own state. (*Con* 65)

These "roots" to a harmonious society are presented step by step as *The Great Digest* stipulates. At the same time, *ben ye* 本业, a term related to *ben* 本, is what Pound emphasized for establishing the social order, appearing again and again in his later cantos, especially the cantos of "The Sacred Edict". *Ben ye* 本业 is used in two senses in *The Cantos*: One is the "fundamental" or "primary" occupation, i.e.

agriculture; the other is one's original calling or profession or "a developed skill from persistence" (Canto XCIX 718). *The Sacred Edict* includes both. Pound immediately grasped the moral theme *ben ye* 本业 — *wu ben ye, yi ding min zhi* 务本业，以定民志 while reading *The Sacred Edit*.

"Food is the root," (Canto XCIX 715) Pound reiterated the government's FIRST job in the "Thrones". Behind food is the economics of agriculture, which is a root occupation for Pound. In a debate about Kung's concern with living rather than death, Pound claimed: "Cemeteries shd. be on high ground, hills least use for cultivation." (*GK* 274) The dead do not need food and thus they should save fields for the living to cultivate. Pound wrote in Canto XCVIII:

> First the pen yeh 本
>
> then τέχνη 業
>
> and to philosophise in old age (Ari's χαθόλου)
> "and that Buddha abandoned such splendours,
> is it likely! " said Yong Tching ...
> Who has seen Taoist priests fly up in broad daylight?
> They destroy the 5 human relations,
> Mules saddled with trappings,
> deeper in debt every day
> and next they are selling their farmsteads.
>
> 佛
>
> And as for these Bhud-foés,
> they provide no mental means for
> Running an empire, nor do taoists
> with their internal and external pills
> — is it external? The gold pill? —
> to preserve them from physical death? (Canto XCVIII 706-707)

Therefore, there is no space for non-fundamental occupations in the society, and those who are not doing *ben ye* 本业 are usurers and bankers in counterpart to traditional Chinese Taoists and Buddhists. In Canto XCIX, he directly warned the people who abandoned agriculture impulsively:

> Don't burn to abandon production and go into trading,
> Dig up root to chase branches (Canto XCIX 730)

Ben ye 本业, for Pound, has a broader meaning which deals with everybody's occupation in the society.

> You, soldiers, civilians,
>
> are not headed to be professors. (Canto XCIX 731)

Everybody should do a job that is well fit for him. Pound criticized those who were soldiers or civilians for trying to be professors. In Pound's opinion, if you are a soldier, you should serve your country when your country needs you because that's your *ben ye* 本业; if you are a civilian, what you ought to do is to cultivate yourself well because that's your *ben ye* 本业. Don't waste your time on the field that does not fit you. If everybody in society could do his own job well, then it is easy to reach a harmonious existence.

Pound himself struggled to find his own *ben ye* 本业. Cheadle (1997: 263) argued: "Study was always essential to Pound; it was his 本业 (*ben ye*) or 'root occupation'." However, Achilles Fang (方志彤), in a letter of March 13, 1952, directly denied Pound's effort in Chinese: "Your DUTY does not exist in Chinese. Modern dix. renders it as pen-fen 本分, which usually means 'one's lot' (as in to be content with one's lot) and i-wu 義務…" (*EPCF* 83). Fang's *ben fen* 本分 is similar to Pound's *ben ye* 本业. It is used by Fang to criticize Pound's interpretation of Confucianism in the monetary reform because that is not his *ben ye* 本业. Maybe that is the starting point of Pound's contemplation of the duty of a man, whether he is an ordinary person or elite. If everyone performs his root occupation and completes it well, is an orderly society far behind?

To conclude this chapter, "order" is what Pound valued most in Confucian ethics. He confidently believed:

> One village in order,
>
> one valley will reach the four seas. (Canto XCIX 729)

5. Pound's Ethics on Man and Nature

5.1 Pound's *Tao* 道 and Nature

Pound considered Confucianism as not only having social ethics dealing with man and community, but also "a totalizing philosophy rooted in the objective reality of organic nature".① The Confucian *Tao* 道② ("the process" often rendered by Pound) operates as an integrated universal principle of the harmonious order of the cosmos or nature: "The celestial and earthly process can be defined in a single phrase; its actions and creations have no duality." (*Con* 183) The human world should be a natural and integrated part of a harmonious cosmos. The human world is a microcosm situated within the macrocosm of the universe itself. Therefore an ideal world should first and foremost follow natural rhythms and be a harmonious part of nature. Pound stated: "The Confucian is totalitarian." (*SP* 85) Little (1982: 156) also argued that it is "primarily for awareness of and interest in totalities, not for total control by government". Pound continued: "Confucius offers a way of life, an Anschauung or disposition toward nature and man and a system for dealing with both." (*GK* 25) But "Greek philosophy was almost an attack upon nature" (*SP* 86).

Pound believed "the sick part of our philosophy is 'Greek splitting'" (*SP* 85) because the Greek philosophers "have been served up as highbrows. We know them as ideas, each handed us as a maxim" (*GK* 23-24).③ As for Pound, that Greek philosophical "splitting" originated from Aristotle. During the years he studied Aristotle's *Metaphysics*, he found:

> Aristotle was banned by the Church, I think because he was so discouraging. Some sort of vital instinct, down under the superficial intolerance and stupidity, felt the menace of logic-chopping, of all this cutting up, rationalizing and dissecting of reality. (*GK* 45)

---

① According to Zhu (2005: 70), Pound's view of nature is influenced by both Neoplatonism and Enlightenment.

② *Dao* in Confucian classics and in *The Cantos* refers to the universe principle inherent in all things — concrete and knowable, not the *Dao* of Daoism.

③ Pound made a distinction between Greek philosophy and Greek mythologies.

Although "Aristotle was banned by the Church", Christianity also could not escape from Pound's denouncement. Pound believed that "Christian thought has never offered a balanced system" (*GK* 29) because the decline of the Church "began with a flight from reality" (*MAW* 133). Therefore, the similarity between Greek philosophy and Christianity lies in the miserable fact that both of them split and cut up "reality". The reality is of organic nature. In Pound's view, Greek mythology didn't commit the "splitting". He held that "Greek philosophy, and European in its wake, degenerated into an attack on mythology" because mythology, in Pound's view, "tries to find an expression for reality without over-simplification, and without scission" (*SP* 87). Mythology, sharing the same characteristic with Confucianism, is "perforce, totalitarian" (*SP* 87). Even though Pound saw an affinity between Eleusinian mysteries and the Confucian society, the Eleusinian elements might be presented in the very early church, but the ancient wisdom "seems to have disappeared when the mysteries entered the vain space of Christian theological discussion" (*SP* 57).

Confucianism is "totalitarian" which means totalizing, no splitting, no chopping, no cutting and no dissecting. It is the *Tao* 道 of nature. Pound remarked:

> The *way* is the process of nature, *one*, in the sense that the chemist and biologist so find it. Any attempt to deal with it as split, is due to ignorance and a failure in the direction of the will. (*SP* 87)

Organic nature is "one", which means no splitting. Any foolhardy behavior against this nature results from "ignorance" and failure towards *zhi* 志 (the will), and leads to loss and death. Pound warned the chemists and biologists: "You can examine a living animal, but at a certain point dissection is compatible only with death." (*SP* 87) What Pound discovered was the essence of traditional Chinese medical skills (*zhong yi* 中医). Weiming Tu sharply criticized those who regarded traditional Chinese medical science as a pseudo-science because they were too ignorant to know *jing luo* 经络, which was the embodiment of living life. Once a person dies, *jing luo* will never exist; therefore, one is doomed never to find *jing luo* when he uses an anatomical method to dissect a dead body (杜维明, 2012: 59). Pound maintained: "At no point does the Confucio-Mencian ethic or philosophy splinter and split away from organic nature." (*SP* 87) Due to Confucianism, he contended: "In the present very imperfect state of half-knowledge I fail to see that the history of China, or Chinese historic process, suffers a dichotomy or split into two opposite forces, as does that of Europe." (*SP* 67)

Pound's discovery of the affinity between the Confucian *Tao* and the mystic philosophical light goes one step further to substantialize the mysterious *Tao* into a visible entity.①

> Reason from heaven, said Tcheou Tun-y
> enlighteneth all things (Canto LV 298)

So the divine and transcendental power becomes a kind of light that shines all things. Pound explicitly stated in an essay written probably in the early 1940s: "Confucian life and thought turns in a world of light and flowing water." (Qtd. in Cheadle, 1997: 102) Pound synthesized the light with Confucian *Tao* at the last part of his translation of *Zhong Yong*:

> *As silky light, King Wen's virtue*
> *Coming down with the sunlight,*
> *what purity!*
> *He looks in his heart*
> *And does.*
> — *Shi King,* IV, I, 2, I.
>
> Here the sense is: In this way was Wen perfect.
> The *unmixed* functions [in time and in space] without bourne.
> This unmixed is the tensile light, the Immaculata. There is no end to its action. (*Con* 187)

A beam of light emanates from the ideogram *xian* 显 (Pound used the complex character "顯"). In this ideogram, Pound saw the light in the Confucian order: The left side of "顯" is silk threads "絲" in the sunshine "日", and the entire character means "display" and "illustrious". A Confucian personification of order, the virtuous King Wen of the Zhou Dynasty is praised as "illustrious" in *Shih-ching: The Classic Anthology Defined by Confucius*. In Pound's etymological vision, he is the embodiment of heavenly intelligence transmitted in the form of light (Tay, 1977: 91).

---

① Liebregts (2004) made a comprehensive study of Pound's involvement with Neoplatonism.

A cluster of Chinese characters associated with light occurred in the later cantos, such as *ming* 明 (bright) for 10 times, *xian* 顯 (manifestation) for 7 times and *dan* 旦 (dawn) for 8 times. Terrell discussed that "*Ming* is central to Pound's idea of divinity manifesting itself through the intelligence of man" (Terrell, 1993: 475). Although *ming* 明 does not play the same important role in Confucianism as Pound postulated, it is true that the character occurs frequently in the "Four Books", linking it to a transcendental power, such as in the introduction to *Tao* 道 in the opening section of *Da Xue* (*ming ming de* 明明德 to illustrate illustrious virtue) and in the description of *tian* 天 in *Zhong Yong* XXVI. 5 (*gao ming* 高明, high and bright). Therefore, Pound considered *ming* 明 as a significant character in Confucianism. Evidence of the importance of this character for Pound is the radical "礻" (The light descending from the sun, moon and stars), which ranks first in the "TERMINOLOGY" and is followed by the character "明". "The sun and moon, the total light process, the radiation, reception, and reflection of light; hence, the intelligence. Bright, brightness, shining. Refer to Scotus Erigena, Grosseteste and the notes on light in my *Cavalcanti*." (*Con* 20) Scotus Erigena, Robert Grosseteste and Guido Cavalcanti all share the analogy of creative light from God (Tay, 1977: 92). Kung is seen as their parallel, possessing a far more pantheistic light.

The light image, a recurrent theme in *The Cantos*, is developed fully and broadly, especially in the later cantos. The linkage of the Confucian *Tao* 道 and Neo-Platonic light recurred in Canto LXXXV:

> Gentlemen from the West,
> Heaven's process is quite coherent
> and its main points perfectly clear.
> 顯 hsien˙ (Canto LXXXV 572)

By juxtaposing "heaven's process" (*tian dao* 天道) and *xian* 顯 (Pound's hsien), the four-line verse conveys three points to his readers. Heaven's process is able to generate light because *xian* 顯 is "tensile light" with the effect of *ming*. Then, the second and third lines depicting heaven's work of generating lives are manifested as a coherent and clear plan of creation. Last but not least, the first line obviously shows that Pound seemed to purposefully address his Western readers. He probably intended to call for Western gentlemen to understand the Confucian *Tao* with the help of Western philosophic light.

Since Pound's philosophical exploration is deeply concerned with nature, then what is nature for Pound? Nature is a beloved topic for Pound, even in his early poems. In Canto XIII, Confucius walked peacefully into the poem:

> KUNG walked
>   by the dynastic temple
> and into the cedar grove,
>   and then out by the lower river (Canto XIII 58)

The opening landscape description has received attention from some Poundian scholars but with more or less different understandings. Qian (2003b: 60) appreciated it from the perspective of Chinese painting, and argued that the Confucian emphasis on "order" was represented in pictures that had impressed Pound. Tay just mentioned casually that the first four lines "form a prologue providing a lyrical atmosphere" (Tay, 1997: 52). And Li (2008: 45) put much importance on this scenic opening. He contended:

> Pound always carefully set the scene for his images in *The Cantos*…his choice of setting in Canto XIII is an important one… Pound embedded Confucius' action in Asian culture: in the numerous temples that have edified people's minds, generation after generation; in the forest that connects people to nature…and in river that washes away the dirt from people's minds and then nurtures and nourishes the healthy growth of the good seed in their hearts.

Admittedly, "the dynastic temple" and "the cedar grove" create a solemn and sacred atmosphere; "the lower river", usually with a tinkling song, provides a kind of relaxed and joyful atmosphere where the mind is at peace with the body. The whole setting depicts a tranquil picture of an environment-friendly life that people live and conveys a hint of beauty and serenity beyond our imagination. The harmonious atmosphere leaves us an impression of the unity possible between humans and nature.

Pound was fascinated by every possible thing in nature, probably due to his strong belief in myths where mysterious power permeates nature, his admiration of Oriental landscape paintings and his fierce love for Chinese nature poetry. Nature leaves numerous footsteps in his poetry. In the prison near Pisa, he observed only minimal traces of nature, including a grasshopper and ants. Meanwhile, he furiously condemned any possible thing that was against nature, such as the visibly formidable environment being shattered and deformed dramatically in the modern world, and also invisible ugliness like usury.

Nature, in Pound's world, not only means mountain, river, wind, dew and so on or bees and ants, but also means "the universe of fluid force" and "the germinal universe of wood alive, of stone alive"; it also means a man is "the sensitive physical part of him" (*SR* 92). "This sense of numinous nature," argued Cookson (2001: 10), "is everywhere present in his greatest poetry and particularly in the later cantos." Pound's concept of nature is in some degree similar to Chinese *tian* 天 usually translated as "heaven". *Tian* 天 is an ambiguous and complex concept in Chinese philosophy. Based on Legge's English translations alone, the Confucian concept of *tian* can yield at least six different meanings in English: a personal deity (*Lun Yu* VI. 26, IX. 5), the transcendental force of creation (*Zhong Yong* XVII. 3), the absolute principles of ethical values (*Lun Yu* VII. 22, XIII. 19), fate (*Lun Yu* XII. 5), the cosmological whole (*Lun Yu* XVII. 19), and the physical sky (*Lun Yu* XIX. 25). The Confucian *tian* can be seen to inscribe dimensions that are at the same time divine and worldly, spiritual and material, eternal and provisional, creating and created.[①] "For Pound, who always longed for a theological paradigm that would overcome the separation between the divine and the human, *tian* seemed to offer an attractive solution." (Lan, 2005: 171).

Tian 天 was neither personalized nor apotheosized by Pound. In the light of Pound's use of three forms of the English word "heaven", Lan (2005: 171) categorized the Confucian *Tian*[②] in Pound's translations into three possible meanings: the divine and intangible entity when *Tian* is rendered as "heaven", the essential force of material reality when *Tian* is translated as "heavens", and something between the infinite and the finite when *Tian* is translated as "heaven". Such categorization is reasonable and acceptable; however, there are actually two basic aspects in Pound's Confucian concept of *Tian* if we pay less attention to his usage of a different form of "heaven" in the translation of *Tian*. Sometimes he did not use "heaven" at all in his translations. For instance, Pound translated Confucius's famous remarks that *Tian* was no more than the non-personal power of nature:

---

① The analysis of Confucian *Tian* 天 is from Lan's (2005: 171) *Ezra Pound and Confucianism — Remaking Humanism in the Face of Modernity*.

② In this book, *Tian* refers to the Confucian 天.

Sky, how does that talk? The four seasons go on, everything gets born. Sky, what words does the sky use? (*Con* 277)

天何言哉，四时行焉，万物生焉，天何言哉？（《论语》XVII. 19）

Does Heaven speak? The four seasons pursue their courses, and all things are continually being produced, but does Heaven say anything? (Legge, 2009: 326)

The divergence of the two versions exists in Pound's and Legge's different translations of *Tian*. "Sky" is not as abstract as heaven, which contains the more transcendental and mystical sense of meaning. Sky is some substance that humans can see and feel so that it is more specific than "heaven". Pound might not weigh the nuance of the two words but just intend to be different from his former translator because he indeed used "heaven" when he conveyed the above idea from *Lun Yu* in one of the "China Cantos" written around the year of 1938:

Reason from heaven, said Tcheou Tun-y
　　　　enlighteneth all things
seipsum seipsum diffundit, risplende
　　　　Is the beginning of all things, et effectu (Canto LV 298)

The significance of the above verse is manifested as follows. It presents the fundamental philosophical doctrine — "reason from heaven" "is the beginning of all things" from the forerunner of the Neo-Confucianism Tcheou Tun-y (周敦颐 Dunyi Zhou, 1017-1073). What Zhou maintains — "reason from heaven", which "is the beginning of all things" — concords with the prominent philosophical idea from *Lun Yu* — "the four seasons go on, everything gets born". As a matter of fact, Zhou's "reason from heaven" is Confucian *Li* 理 (the ultimate principle)① or Confucian *Tao* 道 (the way of heaven). To put it frankly, according to Neo-Confucianism, *Tian* is the origin of every principle (万理之源). *Yuan heng li zhen* 元亨利贞, first put forward by Dunyi Zhou, is the revelation of *Tian* (heaven). It stands for the four seasons, namely spring, summer, autumn and winter. The four seasons closely follow the law of nature and keep going year in and year out, and such natural phenomena well embody

① In Chinese *pinyin* system, the sound of the three characters 理, 礼 and 利 is the same as *li*. In this book, the author uses the capitalized "*Li*" to refer to 理 whenever it appears and the small-letter "*li*" to refer to 礼 and 利. So the *pinyin* "*li*" usually occurs with the latter two Chinese characters standing aside. "*Li*" means 礼 or 利 only when it stands at the beginning of a sentence.

the ultimate principle of the cosmos. This is a typical and representative example of *Li yi fen shu* 理一分殊 (One *Li*, many manifestations; or individual things originating from an ultimate principle). Pound found this law of nature. As Lan (2005: 169-170) argued: "In spite of Pound's recognition of the mysterious nature of the divine force, he believed that divinity manifests itself though the rational ordering of nature, rather than through miracles, particularly of the sort found in the *Old Testament*." Based on "理一分殊", heaven or *Tian* can be interpreted as nature. Moreover, heaven is intimately related to the story of the earth, which, as the habitat of all known creatures, is the proper home for them. Pound vividly described beings created by heaven, such as mountains, rivers and trees in his poetry. Therefore, nature in Poundian Confucianism contained the earthly world and the divine world, namely, earth and heaven.

5.2 The Union with Nature

Pound had a deep concern about man and nature as discussed at the beginning of this section. He believed nature was a broad concept consisting of heaven and earth, and he contended that the Confucian *Li* 理 (the ultimate principle) guaranteed a harmonious existence among heaven, earth and humanity. The Confucian universe is an organic unity in which heaven is the ultimate reality that operates according to a benevolent principle. This principle is the way of heaven that generates all things and brings all things into unity and harmony. What Pound had searched for in his life-long career was the unity of man and nature. Pound commented in the 1931-1932 essay "Terra Italica": "The modern author can write 'aim the union with nature' or 'consciousness of the unity with nature'." (*SP* 59) His exploration of man's union with nature is manifested in two ways: the identity of human nature and things' nature, and the union of the way of heaven and the way of humanity. The former focuses on reestablishing the man-nature relationship which should be "partners" rather than the controller and the controlled; the latter encourages humanity to perceive the universal principle through *ge wu* 格物 (the investigation of things), and calls for humanity to understand the transcendental force known as *Tian* or heaven, and accomplish an inner transcendence through constant self-cultivation.

Pound appreciated Confucius for his anthropocosmic vision of the dynamic interaction among heaven, earth and human. He considered the anthropocosmic vision a vigorous counterforce against the anthropocentric tendency he found in the humanist view cherished by Western intellectuals since the Renaissance. His critical remarks on anthropocentrism appeared as early as 1910 in *The Spirit of Romance*: "After the Treconto we get Humanism, and as the art is carried northward we have Chaucer and Shakespeare, (Jacques-père). Man is concerned with man and forgets the whole and the flowing." (*SR* 93) "The whole and the flowing" means the "vital universe" of things, the world of "fluid force". In the 1921 essay "Axioma", Pound continued to argue: "Concerning the intimate essence of the universe we are utterly ignorant." (*SP* 49) As for Pound, forgetting this world and "ignoring the intimate essence of the universe", no less a sin than forgetting "man" himself, are the clear signs of human beings' alienation from the natural world in which they live.

Actually, Pound's resentment of Western humanism was mostly directly against Christianity. As early as in 1910, Pound evaluated that Christian teaching "is variously and constantly a sort of working hypothesis acceptable to people of a certain range of temperament — a 'regola' which suits a particular constitution of nerves and intellect, and in accord with which the people of this temperament can live at greatest peace with 'the order,' with man and nature" (*SR* 95). In Pound's view, the doctrines of Christianity catered to people of a certain kind of temperament because only this group of people is capable of living harmoniously with man and nature. But Pound searched for a sort of "chivalric love" which may "take on forms interpretive of the divine order" and "lead to an 'exteriorization of the sensibility,' and interpretation of the cosmos by feeling" and aimed at a sort of mind being close on the vital universe (*SR* 93).

One reason that Pound critiqued Christianity is its radical split between the transcendent divine principle and the human world. The separation is manifested in two aspects: humanity's dominance over nature, which is anthropocentrism; God's dominance over humans. Western philosophy, especially after the Renaissance, in Pound's opinion, reinforced this anthropocentric view, which champions human beings as the driving force of progress in history. Christianity holds that human beings are masters of the world and destine to dominate all other creatures of the earth. The great chain of being sheds some light on the role of human beings in the cosmos. According to the Elizabethans, all created things were linked together and arranged in a fixed pattern or chain — the great chain of being (Figure 5-1).

Obviously, at the top of the pyramid rests God who wields the almighty power and is the master of all the living and the dead, including human beings. When compared with God, man is incompetent, ignorant and totally helpless and hopeless.

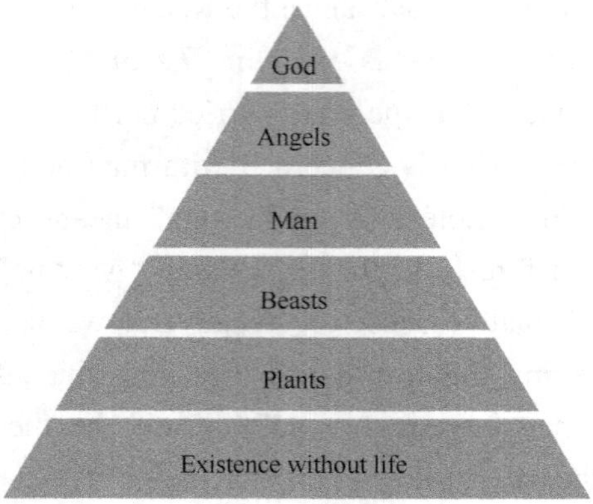

Figure 5-1 The Great Chain of Being

Man loses all his initiative and activity, and becomes completely passive and oppressed. Thus, human beings are separated from the earthly world and the divine world because they do not share an equal position with other beings in the universe so that it is impossible for humanity to have an equal discourse given God's superiority — God is superior to all inferior beings.

But from the Confucian anthropocosmic view, human beings are understood to be embedded in nature rather than being dominant over nature, and everything in nature is interdependent, interrelated, dynamic and transformational. Pound's spiritual ideology of man and nature emerged from his study of mythological paganism in his early poetic years. As noted earlier, Pound was concerned with the relationship of man and nature as early as in 1910 in *The Spirit of Romance*:

> ...the body as pure mechanism. Our kinship to the ox we have constantly thrust upon us; but beneath this is our kinship to the vital universe, to the tree and the living rock." (*SR* 92)

This passage explicitly defines the relationship between man and the vital universe through the word "kinship" and "mechanism". To put it differently, humanity is part of nature and nature is also embedded in humanity. Pound used the word "mechanism" to describe man's role in the universe, and he openly said in the same work: "Man is — the sensitive physical part of him [the universe] — a mechanism". (*SR* 92) Pound, meanwhile, perceived not only man's deep involvement with nature but also the cosmos' embodiment within man because he shortly assumed "the little cosmos 'corresponds' to the greater, that man has in him both 'sun' and 'moon'" (*SR* 94). Moreover, the word "kinship", which stipulates the relationship between man and the universe, postulates the equal status of man and nature rather than the relationship of a ruler and his domain.

Pound's view of the universe — the "fluid force", "the living rock", etc. — is explicitly presented in "Section: The Rock-Drill":

> By the nymphs ... and have ecstasy, sober
> and that the universe is alive
> ἐρωτά ιοχει (Canto XCIV 657)

The first two lines depict a truly harmonious universe in which "the music of the spheres, or, the harmony flowing in the cosmos, is part of the *forma* or the *concetta*" and "the song of the nymphs in ecstasy fulfills true harmony" (Terrell, 1993: 578). The Greek word "ἐρωτά" means "love it has...and knits together", which conveys an implication that the universe "fulfills the role of mother and father...; and it is possessed by a love for itself more intense than any separate being has for its fellows, a passion which knits it together into harmony" (Terrell, 1993: 577). This poetic line shows a striking philosophic similarity with the famous remarks of Zai Zhang 张载, a prominent Chinese philosopher in the Song Dynasty:

> *Qian* (*Tian* or heaven) is my father and *Kun* (earth) is my mother. As a trivial being, I stand between them. Therefore, all things created by heaven are my body; and the principle of heaven is my innate nature. All people are my brothers and sisters; and all things are my companions.①
>
> 乾称父，坤称母；予兹藐焉，乃混然中处。故天地之塞，吾其体；天地之帅，吾其性。民，吾同胞；物，吾与也。

Zai Zhang has great importance in Confucianism. The similarity between Pound's poetic verse and Zai Zhang's statement offers strong evidence of Pound's profound understanding of Confucianism. Pound doubtless recognized the word "I" contains a sense of security rather than a sense of alienation although "I" is insignificantly small in the scope of a capacious nature. Pound's recognition of a human kinship to nature envisions the identity between the nature of humanity and the nature of things.

The perception of a man-nature relationship was deepened when Pound translated

① It's from Zai Zhang's work *Xi Ming* (《西铭》). The author of this book translated the Chinese into English.

the Confucian work *Zhong Yong*:

> Only the most absolute sincerity under heaven can bring the inborn talent to the full and empty the chalice of the nature.
>
> He who can totally sweep clean the chalice of himself can carry the inborn nature of others to its fulfillment; getting to the bottom of the natures of men, one can thence understand the nature of material things, and this understanding of the nature of things can aid the transforming the nutritive powers of earth and heaven [ameliorate the quality of the grain, for example] and raise man up to a sort of third *partner* with heaven and earth. (*Con* 173.5 [Italic mine])

This passage points two significant ideas: The absolute sincerity (*zhi cheng* 至诚) is the only possible means to achieve an ideal state of being, which will be explained shortly; man is raised to "a sort of third *partner* with heaven and earth". The changing of the core from "kinship" to "partner" is profound in meaning. The word "partner" indicates Pound's sight into the man-nature relationship. It indicates co-workers, cooperation and co-action to highlight the positive participation of man in nature. Tu (杜维明, 2012: 106) shared a similar attitude toward man's role in nature with Pound. He maintained:

> In the Confucian view, man is not only the observer and appreciator, but, at the same time, a participator, a creator and even a destroyer.①

The word "participator", which is similar to Pound's "partner", highlights the active role of human beings, and Tu explicitly defined the human role as either a positive creator or a negative destroyer. Pound coincidently called for human beings "to be men not destroyers" in the "Draft and Fragment" (823). He saw the destructive power of human beings thoroughly while underlining the creative power of humanity. Man's destruction of nature is well manifested especially in the "Hell Cantos" (Canto XIV-Canto XV) and the "Usura Canto" (Canto XLV).

The "Hell Cantos" begins with "Io venni in luogo d'ogni luce muto (I came to a place utterly without light); / The stench of wet coal, politicians" (Canto XIV 61). The place that man has destroyed is totally dark, and smells badly; what's more, here "flies carrying news, harpies dripping sh-t through the air", "the soil living pus, full of vermin, / dead maggots begetting live maggots", and finally Pound may find the

① The translation is done by the author of this book.

canker — "monopolist" who is the obstructor of knowledge and the obstructor of distribution (Canto XIV 63). The "monopolist" refers to the usurer who is sharply blamed by Pound as "sin against nature" (Canto XLV 229). This theme is fully developed in Canto XLV:

> Azure hath a canker by usura
> ...
> Usura slayeth the child in the womb
> It stayeth the young man's courting
> It hath brought palsey to bed, lyeth
> between the young bride and her bridegroom
> CONTRA NATURAM
> They have brought whores for Eluesis
> Corpses are set to banquet
> at behest of usura. (Canto XLV 230)

Rather like heaven that gives life to all things, usura is vehemently impeached by Pound for the fact that it brings only death and sterility. So Pound employed the Latin words written in capital letters "CONTRA NATURAM" to lay stress on the sin of usura — against nature. Besides killing "the child in the womb", usura deprives the young bride and her bridegroom of sex by bringing "palsey to bed". Sex is for productivity and entertainment. On the one hand, the young bride has no chance to produce a child because of her inability to have sex; on the other hand, whores can have sex but cannot conceive. By bringing whores to Eluesis, which is a representative of harvest, usura kills the last opportunity of producing life. It's obvious that Pound hated usura because he realized its purpose was to produce only more money and produced nothing with any real value.

Thus, Pound had an urgent need for a harmonious relationship between humanity and nature. Pound believed that human beings are not merely creatures, but co-creators of the cosmic process. As co-creators, human beings work with heaven and earth in a symbiotic relationship to create harmonious societies. Therefore, a command of the identity between the nature of humanity and the nature of things is not enough for human beings to attain harmony between man and nature. To achieve the ideal existence of being, man must come to know nature intimately and self-cultivate constantly.

The beginning of self-cultivation is *ge wu* 格物 (the investigation of things), which is from Pound's beloved Confucian classic *Da Xue*. The "completion of knowledge is rooted" in *ge wu* 格物, which is translated by Pound into "sorting things into organic categories" (*Con* 31). Actually, it is the basis of the realization of humanity's moral nature upon which the attainment of the social order and harmony depends. Knowledge of natural law will make the process intelligible, and the "understanding of the principle in external things would ultimately lead to an understanding of the principle within oneself" (Zhu, 2006: 397). Therefore, not only to know the law of nature (*Tao* 道 [the way of heaven]) but also to hold ample respect for nature are essential to accomplishing the unity of *tian dao* 天道 (the way of heaven) and *ren dao* 人道 (the way of man). Moreover, incessant self-cultivation is crucial in the process.

Knowledge of natural law is attained by "sorting things into organic categories" (*ge wu* 格物). Nature, for Pound, is an organic reality that could not be split. The universe, as one entity, works and operates in accordance with a central and benevolent principle, which is Confucian *Li* 理 or *Tao* 道. To know the principle, man must understand that the world of things is an organic whole, full of living spirits sustained by the same inviolable laws of dynamic creations.

Pound was not an atheist; he believed the existence of gods. "I assert that the Gods exist," He declared, "and this very simple sentence leaves Mr. Eliot just as much in the dark as he was asking: What Mr. P. believes." (*GK* 299) As noted earlier, he vehemently critiqued religions, especially Christian, so there was no surprise in T. S. Eliot questioning Pound's beliefs. Actually, Pound's God is not the Christian God but the supreme creative force. "The invisible supreme force of creation that unifies all finite beings in its absolute reality." (Lan, 2005: 169) Although Pound occasionally used the word "God" to refer to the divine force, he at times employed other phrases to mention it, such as "eternal state of mind", "*theos*", "intimate essence", "luminous principle of Reason" or the Neoplatonic "*nous*". The various terms for the same entity revealed his attempt to redefine this transcendental category in unconventional terms, and his difficulty in capturing an unorthodox theological vision in a single term or phrase.

It's the monotheism of Christianity that motivated Pound's dislike of the Christian God. He admitted: "It is, however, impossible to prove whether the *theos* be one or many." (*SP* 51) But he reiterated: "My emphasis is on the plural" because "a god in the singular is always lacking in temperance, in amenity, a god in the singular is on the whole, a peril, an imminent nuisance" (*MAW* 135). In Pound's view, "the greatest tyrannies have arisen from the dogma that the *theos* is one, or that there is a unity above various strata of *theos* which imposes its will upon the sub-strata, and thence upon human individuals" (*SP* 51). Therefore, a man who believes in one God is doomed to be a slave of the dogma and becomes silent and voiceless in his spiritual domain "for the lack of gods (plural) man suffers, or let us say he very gradually impoverishes his mind by the elimination of irreplaceable concepts" (*MAW* 135). In Pound's poems, a variety of gods from the East and West appear on the poetic stage, including Kuanon (*Guanyin*) from Chinese Buddhism and the moon goddess Artemis from Greek mythologies.

From the 1920s to the early 1940s, Pound questioned Western orthodox religious beliefs and philosophy, but his own philosophic ideas did not take a systematic form. Pound expressed the difficulties he was having in his investigation of transcendental power: "We have no proof that this God, *Theos*, is one or is many, or is divisible or indivisible, or is an ordered hierarchy culminating, or not culminating, in a unity." (*SP* 49) Nevertheless, his spiritual position at that time took on a discernible shape through his exploration of European pagan mythologies. Pound strictly distinguished which states of mind were gods and which were not.

> Are all eternal states of mind gods?
> We consider them so to be.
> Are all durable states of mind gods?
> They are not. (*SP* 47)

The difference between the English words "eternal" and "durable" lies in the fact that the former is something "infinite" while the later "finite". That is to say, to become gods, one needs to know and perceive the infinite universe. Two breakthroughs come in Pound's philosophical exploration. One breakthrough is that the divine force is the ultimate source of life, and it manifests itself through the rational ordering of nature, a striking parable with the Confucian doctrine *Li yi fen shu* 理一分殊. The second breakthrough occurred during Pound's quest of "When does a man become a god?" and his answer was enlightened — "When he enters one of these states of mind." (*SP*

47). A man is capable of becoming a god when he enters the eternal states of mind. Furthermore, "the god has at last succeeded in becoming human, and it is not the beauty of the god but the personality which is the goal of the love and the invocation" (*SR* 98), premising Confucians' inner transcendence through self-cultivation.

5.3 The Transcendental Power: "Their Sealed Order"

Transcendental power or the immanent divinity in Confucianism is *ming* 命 or *tian ming* 天命, customarily translated as the "heavenly mandate" or the "mandate of heaven". Pound rendered it differently according to various Confucian contexts, such as "sealed orders" (*Con* 244) or a similar phrase "what heaven has disposed and sealed", sometimes "the order of heaven" (*Con* 198), and even simply "destiny" (*Con* 228). According to the end of *The Unwobbling Pivot* XVII, "who has this great power to see clearly into himself without tergivisation [sic], and act thence, will come to his destiny (that is a high destiny)". *Tian ming* 天命 contains political meanings and inner transcendence. As for the political sense, Wu Wang 武王 (King Wu) is legitimately the first emperor to accept the mandate of heaven to overthrow the tyranny of the despot Zhou Wang 纣王 (Pound's Chou or Cheou).

Tian ming 天命 or *ming* 命 is a recurrent theme in Pound's epic *The Cantos*. The Chinese character "命" appeared in "Section: Rock-Drill":

> Cdn't see it (ming) could
>
> 命 extend to the people's subsidia[①],
>
> that it was in some fine way tied up with the people (Canto LXXXV 578)

Ming 命, in Terrell's explanation, is the "will of God" or "life-destiny" which is coincident with the meaning of Pound's philosophical term *tian ming*. What is crucial for a ruler is not only to receive the mandate of heaven but also to govern wisely and support his people, wherein *ming* or divinity also "manifests in the intelligence of all man great or small" (Terrell, 1993: 479). However, if the ruler does not follow natural justice and governs corruptly, heaven may punish him, and this idea is expressed through the character *zhen* 震 (Pound's chên):

> non coelum non in medio

① "Subsidia" means "support".

but man is under Fortuna
? that is a forced translation?
La donna che volgo
Man under Fortune,

CHêN 震 (Canto LXXXVI 586)

Here, the first line, according to Xie (1999: 218), "is a quotation from Séraphin Couvreur's Latin version of the Chinese *Shu Ching* (*The Book of History*) in the context of an admonition to the wise ruler: the idea that Heaven deals impartially with everything". Pound, with full awareness of "a forced translation", rendered *ming* 命 as "but man is under Fortuna" linking Chinese *ming* and the European Goddess of Fortuna because both are efficacious in human affairs (individual or governmental). "The ideogram, *chên*, denotes for Pound the thundering action from Heaven signifying divine punishment for corrupt government and for deviation from the process of natural justice." (Xie, 1999: 218) The "China Cantos" depict the rise and decline of Chinese dynasties. When the ruler follows the mandate of heaven, it waxes; while when the ruler does not, it wanes.

Therefore, a conclusion was naturally drawn — Pound respected and supported the order of heaven. In the "TERMINOLOGY" preceding the Confucian text, the term *bao you ming* 保佑命 is listed with the interpretation "nourishing, supporting the destiny" (*Con* 23). Such an inspiring understanding of *tian ming* may derive from his translation of *Lun Yu*. Confucius's doctrine of *wei tian ming* 畏天命 (respect the mandate of heaven) must have been impressed on Pound's mind for he rendered: "The proper man...stands in awe of the decrees of destiny [heaven's mouth and seal]." (*Con* 271) Pound's strong belief in *ming* is manifested in his attitude to the fabricated charge of treason. Pound was translating *Meng Zi* (*Mencius*) of the "Four Books" when he was taken away by Italian partisans on 3 May 1945. This work continued even when he was moved to the DTC. Lieutenant Colonel Steele, the commander at the DTC, wrote in a letter to his mother on 20 August 1945:

> "Instead of spending his many spare moments organizing whatever he may think he has for a defense for his case, he spends his time pottering away at a translation of Menghis [Mencius], the Chinese philosopher" (private collection). (*EDP* 48)

Pound was still immersed in Confucian philosophic translation and writing rather than preparing for a defense for his case. Was Pound not anxious for his life and his fate?

As everybody knows, when someone is convicted of treason, he is probably sentenced to death. However, Pound might have more confidence in his fate because he believed "death and life have their sealed orders, riches and honours are from heaven" (*Con* 244). This is *si sheng you ming, fu gui zai tian* 死生有命，富贵在天 (*Lun Yu* XII. 5). Probably that's the reason why he didn't spend his time on defense for his case.

Another important reference to *tian ming* in *The Cantos* is the Chinese character *ling* 灵 (靈) translated by Pound usually as "sensibility". Pound's translation of this word shows his strong concern with humanity — such a quality distinguishes man from animals. As for Pound, he concluded that the "record of Confucius is the record of a very great sensibility" (*GK* 255). The picturesque character on the top of the first page of Canto LXXXV behaves like a heavenly rule, guiding the tendency of "our dynasty". Pound reiterated *ling* 靈 — "our dynasty came in because of a great sensibility" — twice more (Canto LXXXV 571, 575). "Our dynasty" refers to the Shang Dynasty in which the last king Cheou (Zhou Wang 纣王) lost his sovereignty to King Wu because of his immoral administration and his impertinence to heaven. In Canto LXXXV (572), Pound wrote: "Ling^2 靈 / was basis of the rule." He used the character "靈" to bind together the processes of heaven with the processes of nature as well as the Confucian ideals of order in man. The sky-cloud component on the top of this character, with three rain-drops in the middle and "巫" referring to the earth-ceremonies at the bottom, connotes a kind of man-nature harmony — the processes of heaven's will are reflected in the actions of an emperor who treats the people well.

Pound's quest for immanent benevolence is also manifested in his interpretation of *Tao* 道 (Pound's process) and his another beloved Chinese character *zhong* 中 (Pound's pivot). His insights into two of the crucial Confucian doctrines come from his translation of *Zhong Yong* (Pound's *The Unwobbling Pivot*). *Tao* 道 is a complicated concept in Chinese philosophy. For Pound, its meaning is something that originates in heaven and completes itself in human beings. What appeals to Pound lies in his discovery of the affinity between the Confucian "道" and the Neo-Platonic philosophy of light at the end of *The Unwobbling Pivot. Zhong* 中, originating from the doctrine *zhong yong* 中庸, and this becomes a recurrent theme in the later cantos.

The intimacy of *tian ming* and *Tao* is manifested in Pound's translation of the opening passage of *Zhong Yong*:

> What heaven has disposed and sealed is called the inborn nature. The realization of

> this nature is called the process. The clarification of this process [the understanding or making intelligible of this process] is called education. (*Con* 99)

> 天命之谓性，率性之谓道，修道之谓教。(《中庸》I. 1)

The succinct translation shows Pound's fairly exact understanding of the inherent relationship of the mandate of heaven (天命), the inborn nature (性), and education (教). Only does one's continual self-cultivation enable him to complete his inborn nature can he achieve the ultimate principle. Pound usually used "the process" to refer to *Tao* 道. And he defined *Tao* in the "TERMINOLOGY" preceding the Confucian translations: "The process. Footprints and the foot carrying the head; the head conducting the feet, an orderly movement under lead of the intelligence." (*Con* 22) *Tao* in Chinese philosophy is something transcendental and mysterious; however, Pound's "process" is easy for readers, especially Western readers, to understand. He even embodied it with some corporeal organs, such as "having a head and feet", for his translation in *Da Xue* reads: "To know what precedes and what follows, is nearly as good as having a head and feet."① (*Con* 29) *Tao* is to have a head and feet and is to know what precedes and what follows. To know what precedes and what follows is the order of nature. If one behaves or acts in accordance with this natural order or natural law, one has access to *Tao* 道 (the process). He sometimes translated it as "ethic" which was much less mystical and laid stress on the moral that the Confucian *Tao* begins with common people and reaches into heaven. As an ethic or process, the Confucian *Tao* is accessible to all.

5.4 Man in Nature: *Jing*, *Cheng* 敬，诚

The urgent requirement for a man living in the universe is to fully respect nature. Pound highlighted the Chinese character "敬" (reverse, respect). Besides the meaning of respect for the elder in the former chapter, this word also conveys a kind of respect for nature and the law of nature. This character appears not just once in *The Cantos*: "敬 ching / in the 4th / tone / To respect the vegetal powers." (Canto LXXXVII 601-602) He defined it in the preceding section of *The Analects*: "Respect for the kind of intelligence that enables grass seed to grow grass; the cherry-stone to make cherries." (*Con* 193) This power also occurs in *The Cantos*:

① The Chinese version of Pound's translation goes as follows: *zhi suo xian hou ze jin dao yi* 知所先后则近道矣.

> "We have", said Mencius, "but phenomena."
> monumenta. In nature are signatures
> needing no verbal tradition,
> oak leaf never plane leaf. John Heydon. (Canto LXXXVII 593)

Pound advocated "Observe[ing] the phenomena of nature as one in whom the ancestral voices speak" (*Con* 215-216) so that "he makes us see again a beauty that has always been there; that the world has forgotten it does not make it any less real" (*SP* 10). The intelligence in nature rests on the fact that it just goes on but does not speak, and the colours of leaves are signatures in nature. Here it is a kind of intelligence in nature that makes an acorn produce only an oak tree rather than a plane. Pound juxtaposed the Chinese sage Mencius and the English astrologer John Heydon. John Heydon was later called by Pound as the "secretary of nature" (Canto XCI 631). In the first version of Canto III, Pound devoted 23 lines to him, calling him a "worker of miracles", a visionary and a "servant of God and secretary of nature" (Terrell, 1993: 495). As for Mencius, Pound liked Mencius's parable — "the man who pulled up his corn because it didn't grow fast enough, and then told his family he had assisted the grain" (*SP* 87). In *The Cantos*, Pound explicitly referred to it with three eye-catching vertical Chinese characters:

> 勿
> 助
> 長
> as it stands in the Kung-Sun Chow. (Canto LXXXIII 552)

The three characters that mean "do not assist (the grain) grow" give a warning that human beings should respect the law of nature, and any anti-nature behavior will result in harm to nature and self-destruction.

"Peace comes of good manners" (Canto XCIX 718) and such peace expects the law of nature. The law is *fa* 法 in Chinese. Pound wrote:

> Heaven, man, earth, our law as written
> not outside their natural colour,
> water, earth and biceps, fa$^{3-5}$ lu 法 (Canto XCIX 718-719)

Terrell interpreted: "Now in the laws and statures there are a thousand sections...and none go beyond the measure of affection and the calculation of reason." (Terrell, 1993: 639) This short poetic verse, actually, indicates Pound strong intention to affiliate heaven, man and earth, and his high awareness that man must perforce adhere to the law which is written on "water, earth and biceps" to regulate organic nature. Pound's explanation of "law" is unique and hits the crucial point, embodying the affiliation between man and nature. Such a marvelous poetic line resulted from his ideogrammic translation of the Chinese character 法 which has three components: 氵= "water"; 土= "earth"; 厶= "biceps". *Fa* 法 is also "the calculation of reason" which is *Li* 理 (the ultimate principle).

To follow natural law is the realization of *Tao* 道 (the process), finally reaching an ideal state called *zhong yong* 中庸. Pound defined *zhong* 中 (namely his *chung*) and *yong* 庸 (namely his *yung*) in this way:

> The word *chung* signifies what is bent neither to one side nor to the other. The word *yung* signifies unchanging. What exists plumb in the middle is the just process of the universe and that which never wavers or wobbles is the calm principle operant in its mode of action. (*Con* 97)

The concept of *chung yung* is one of the most important qualities of the "calm principle" of the universe. This "calm principle" is Pound's translation of Zhu Xi's concept of *Li* 理, and the process of the universe is his translation of the Confucian *Tao* 道, the fundamental working of the universe. *Zhong* 中 or *pivot* is "the great root of the universe" (*Con* 103). *Zhong* 中 is also a recurring motif in *The Cantos*, and the character appears eight times since Canto LXX. The Confucian notion of *zhong yong* first enters in *The Cantos* as early as in lines 56-58 of Canto XIII. A man who is capable of standing firm in the middle is *jun zi* 君子 or *ren zhe* 仁者. Pound described this man in *Zhong Yong*:

> ...sincere man finds the axis without forcing himself to do so. He arrives at it without thinking and goes along naturally in the midst of the process [Ts'ung yung ching tao], he is a wise man. He who is sincere seizes goodness, gripping it firmly from all sides. (*Con* 167-169)

Only the most sincere man can arrive at *zhong yong zhi dao* 中庸之道 (Pound's Ts'ung yung ching tao). The emperor Shun is "a great and uprising knower". "He observed their discordant motives and followed the middle line between these inharmonic extremes in governing the people, thus he deserved his name." (*Con* 107) *Zhong* is a balanced force to avoid running to any extreme. Pound stated: "I am for balance 中 / and know not how it is but mankind have an aversion." (Canto LXX 413) In this sense, *zhong* is similar to *Tao* 道.

Therefore, what man is concerned with is how to stand firm in the middle or how to realize internal transcendence — a connection with heaven. In his spiritual quest, Pound found the importance of *cheng* 诚 (sincerity) again and the power behind it — *xin* 心 (heart or mind). Although its significance has been discussed before, *cheng* 诚 is crucial in the identity of heaven's way and man's way. The significance of *cheng* is distinctly stated in *Zhong Yong*: "Sincerity is the way of heaven. The attainment of sincerity is the way of men." (Legge, 2009: 413) "Only the most absolute sincerity under heaven can effect any change." The man who has it will be raised up "to be a sort of third partner with heaven and earth". Pound believed that "the nature of things is good" (*SP* 87). Thus when one's moral virtues are in tune with things he is able to foreknow — "arrive at a knowledge of what will occur" (Makin, 2005: 174). And Pound wrote: "In this sense absolute sincerity has the power of a spiritual being, it is like a *numen*." (*Con* 175-177)

Cheng 诚 (sincerity), according to Pound, comes from the real or sincere voice from *xin* 心 (heart or mind). Pound highlighted the importance of *xin* 心 in the union of man and nature. In the 1938 book *Guide to Kulchur*, Pound expressed a kind of supernatural tendency of the union: "There are three modes of thought, cogitation, meditation, and contemplation…in the third [the mind] is unified with the object." (*GK* 77) In Canto XCI, particular stress on *zheng xin* 正心 (Pound's rectifying the heart) is a recurrent demand. He blamed *dao shi* 道士 (Pound's Taosers) of being "concerned neither with heaven, earth / or with anything on the square / but wholly subjective" (Canto XCI 716), and critiqued Buddhism because it did not concern itself with anything in the four corners of the universe:

> Of heaven, earth and of things without shadows,
> Cut the cackle and do not believe 'em.
> Better physical poison than brain wash
>   hsin^{1} shu$^{4-5}$
>   hai^{4}
> The mind at the start had
>   cheng^{4} (Canto XCIX 721)

"Brain wash" is even worse than "physical poison". Pound denounced those who "hsin^{1} shu$^{4-5}$ hai^{4}" 心术坏 (meaning the mind or heart is not good) so that Pound exhorted time after time: "The mind at the start had cheng^{4} (*zheng* 正 upright, rectify)." Pound's emphasis of *zheng xin* in the latter cantos is predicted in his translation of *Da Xue*, which stresses "self-discipline is rooted in rectifying the heart" (*Con* 53). He clarified the relationships of "a good job", "honesty", "good manners" and "tuan^{1} cheng^{4}" (rectifying the heart 端正). All of these lead to "good living".

> Let a man do a good job at his trade,
> whence is honesty;
> whence are good manners,
> good custom
> This is tuan^{1} cheng^{4}
> good living (Canto XCIX 720)

Unlike the absolute concern with the heart in Buddhism, Confucian heart theory, developed mainly by Mencius and Yangming Wang was highly eulogized by Pound. One evidence is *si duan* 四端, which are four dispositions and four kinds of innate good nature of human beings. The other proof is that, besides *cheng* 诚 (the true voice from the heart), Pound laid great importance on some Chinese characters related to the character *xin* 心, such as *de* 德, *zhi* 志, *shen* 慎 and *xin* 信, all introduced in the "TERMINOLOGY". Pound contended that "tien t'ang^{2} hsin^{1} li$^{3-5}$ (heaven's temple is in the heart) in Canto XCIX. But it is quite different from the Buddhist belief that Buddha sits in the heart of the pious because Confucians not only concern themselves with the heart, but also:

> Confucians observe the weather,
> hear thunder,
> seek to include. (Canto XCI 722)

Confucianism appeals to Pound because Confucians not only take care of the heart, but also concern themselves with the universe and search for inclusiveness.

The heart's positive role is manifested in cultivating the *hao ran zhi qi* 浩然之气 (grand air) presented by Pound in Canto LXXXIII:

> this breath wholly covers the mountains

> it shines and divides
> it nourishes by its rectitude
> does no injury
> overstanding the earth it fills the nine fields
> to heaven
>
> Boon companion to equity
> it joins with the process
> lacking it, there is inanition.
>
> When the equities are gathered together
> as birds alighting
> it springeth up vital
>
> If deeds be not ensheaved and garnered in the heart
> there is inanition (Canto LXXXIII 551)

These lines are from *Meng Zi* II. 1.2 in which Mencius talked with his disciples about *hao ran zhi qi* — something cultivated within the self through the consistent accumulation of righteous deeds. Even Mencius said it's difficult to describe, but here Pound depicted this abstract philosophic concept in a 14-line poetic verse. On the one hand, the extremely large (大) and exceedingly strong (刚) air fill up all between heaven and earth. It is the "boon companion" to equity or righteousness. When it is brotherhood to equity, it is in accordance with *Tao* 道. Without it, man is in a state of starvation. On the other hand, *hao ran zhi qi* is attained through an incessant commitment to equity. Accident accumulation of acts of righteousness could not result in the accomplishment of it. Man's heart must be satisfied with his conduct, or his human nature will be starved. The last thing that is worth mentioning is Pound's translation of the term. Compared with Legge's translation as "passion nature", Pound's "breath" is more corporeal because Pound valued the human body and claimed "the body is inside" (Canto XCIX 720), i.e. "the body is inside the soul" (Canto CXIII 808). Pound compared nature to a sacred substance with life that enabled one to breathe. "His horse's mane flowing / His body and soul are at peace." (Canto CI 747) As one with himself, he is one with the cosmos.

Part III Pound's Confucianism and the Modern World

"Kung's life appears to be in conformity with the best modern views. I suspect that a minority has always held these views." (*GK* 272)

6. Pound's Confucianism as a Remedy for Western Disease

In the year of 1937, just on the eve of World War II, Pound appealed for an "immediate need of Confucius" as a cure for what he had diagnosed as a Western disease, i.e., "Western disease shows in sixty percent racket on ink money" (*SP* 76). He reiterated: "That is a *symptom* of moral obtuseness." (*SP* 76) The "sixty percent racket on ink money" refers to usury — what Pound repeatedly and vehemently attacked with every possible opportunity in his prose, poetry, etc. Furthermore, usury in Pound's view has been partially responsible for the "moral and spiritual bankruptcy" of the church (*MAW* 133). On the one hand, the church could not attract people to church on Sundays because people lost faith in Christ due to ambiguous new ideologies, the challenge of modern science and the destruction of world wars. This led to man's alienation from the self, society and nature in the Western world. On the other hand, Christianity itself was deficient in three aspects: the lack of respect for individuality, little concern with ethics, and an attack on nature. Therefore, Christianity is impotent to solve the problems plaguing Western society. Pound turned to Confucianism instead to find a power that could cure the Western world's "moral obtuseness" and alienation.

Pound's Confucian medicine is well manifested in his ideas regarding man and self, his ethics on man and society, and his ethics on man and nature. Pound's ideas regarding man and self concentrate on self-cultivation, which means how to become a "real man" (*ren zhe* 仁者). In 1840, John Stuart Mill warned: "At present individuals are lost in the crowd." (Qtd. in Morgan, 1942: 434) Pound emphasized this same worry as well. In 1927, Pound believed a serious problem in "the tendency to mess into other people's affairs before establishing order in one's own affairs" (*SP* 216). As for Pound, Confucius's respect for the nature of the individual and his emphasis on "establishing order within oneself" serve as the best antidote against Western self-alienation (*SP* 216).

Pound's ethics on man and society deal with the relationship between the individuals and the state. It cured Western social-alienation, a lack of belonging. Since

Christianity has little concern with ethics, Pound found that the power of Confucian ethics rests on defining people's social positions so that each person fits properly. Although the personal order is established through self-cultivation, the purpose of Confucian self-cultivation is to train a person to be a good social being. Since man's social relations begin with the family, Pound maintained that *xiao ti* 孝悌 played an essential role in developing proper relations within the family. At the same time, *li* 礼 and *jing* 敬 are indispensable for establishing a balanced social order. Pound put special emphasis on *zheng ming* 正名 which is *jun jun chen chen fu fu zi zi* 君君臣臣父父子子 in terms of social relations. For the elite and the ordinary people, Pound put forward different demands. As for the elite, i.e. the head of a state, Pound's concept of *ren zhe* is *wang wang* 王王 ("king king", which means that a king should behave like a king). A good king is the one who knows how to spend his treasury rather than enrich it. As for the ordinary people, what Pound stressed is that citizens should do the jobs that best fit them (*ben ye* 本业) so as to keep good relations within social groups.

Pound's ethics on man and nature run against the Christian attack on nature and usury, which is totally "CONTRA NATURAM" (Canto XLV 230). Different from the Christian anthropocentric view, Confucian philosophy is anthropocosmic, i.e., human beings are embedded in nature rather than being dominant over nature. As a totalitarian philosophy, Confucianism emphasizes the idea that the universe has an organic nature. Man, as an indispensable part of nature, ought to respect the law of nature (*Tao* 道, *Li* 理). Any actions that are against nature will result in self-destruction. Pound's concept of nature shares some similarities with the Confucian *Tian* 天, which is well represented in *yuan heng li zhen* 元亨利贞. One particular trait of *Tian* is that everything is generated as the four seasons go on. Usury, however, cannot produce anything with a real value apart from "ink money".

Ezra Pound prescribed his particular brand of Confucian medicine for the disease he diagnosed eating away in the West. Some readers might be critical enough to check the effectiveness of this medicine, and find out that Pound's medicine was of no use in preventing or stopping World War II and to prevent or cool down the Cold War. However, as a poet, translator and critic, rather than a high official in the government, Pound exerted limited influence on social reforms. Pound knew this point well and could only try and visit Benito Mussolini and Winston Churchill so as to discuss his ideas.[①] So it's unrealistic to judge the effectiveness of his views from the point of social improvement because he's neither a statesman nor a social reformer although he made a multitude of comments on politics and economics. But who can neglect Pound's influence? Theoretically, Pound was a good "doctor" because he prescribed a special medicine for the diseases of the West. Practically, his advocating of Confucianism means a lot to the maintenance and transmission of Confucian thoughts in both the Occidental and Oriental worlds.

① On January 30, 1933, Ezra Pound met with Benito Mussolini. Such a brief meeting led to Pound's personal disaster — his imprisonment for 13 years. Pound was so impressive after the meeting that he reported he had "never met anyone who seemed to GET my ideas so quickly as the boss" (see https://www.poemhunter.com/ezra-pound/biography/). However, Pound's request to visit Winston Churchill was rejected in 1939.

7. The Legacy of Pound's Confucianism

Pound's fascination with Confucianism received attention in the West when he was alive, and continued after his death. The study of Pound's involvement with Confucianism kept abreast with the study of Pound's poetry, translation, literary theories, etc. Scholars who have contributed to this study include Achilles Fang, Hugh Kenner and L. S. Dembo. Their studies may not be systematic enough, but they nevertheless shed great light on the subject of this book. The influence of Pound's Confucianism should not be ignored, and the author will explore it in three fields: Poundian scholarship, Confucian scholarship and amateur readers. There is also a tentative exploration of Pound's Confucianism and modern China at the end of the chapter.

7.1 Poundian Scholarship

Pound should be read "in context"① and Pound's life-long involvement with Confucianism has become an essential and indispensable factor when we read Pound. It has reached a consensus in Poundian scholarship that the study of Ezra Pound is not complete without reading him from the view of Confucianism. John J. Nolde (1986: 90) argued: "EP [Ezra Pound] thought he was a Confucian and wrote from this perspective. His writings make sense only if this is understood." Pound's Confucianism paved a new way to understand *The Cantos*, his ideas on politics and economics as well as his Chinese translations.

Confucianism is an inseparable part in *The Cantos*. Pound introduced Confucius (Pound's Kung) in Canto XIII and started Confucius's journey in the epic. Pound preferred "Kung" to "Confucius" in *The Cantos*. And in Canto XIII, "Kung" is the only name that Pound addressed the Chinese sage, which shows up 10 times. In the later cantos, Pound sometimes addressed him "Kungfutseu" ("Kung-fu-tseu" or "Kung fu tseu"), sometimes "Confucius", and even directly called his courtesy name "Chung Ni", together with the Chinese characters "仲尼". In Canto LIII, Pound officially

① Nadel edited a book and named it *Ezra Pound in Context*.

introduced Confucius in this way:

> This was the year of the two eclipses
> And Cheou-lang that held up the portcullis
> was named 'hillock' because of a lump on his head
> Man of Sung, and his line of Lou land **Chung** 仲
> and his second son was **Kung-fu-tseu**
> Taught and the not taught. **Kung** and Eleusis
> to catechumen alone.
> And when **Kung** was poor, a supervisor of victuals
> Pien's report boosted him **Ni** 尼
> so that he was made supervisor of cattle
> In that time were banquets as usual, **Kung** was inspector of
> markets[1] (Canto LIII 272)

The poetic lines start with the year when Confucius was born and his father's heroic conduct — "held up the portcullis". "Cheou-lang" is Kung's father — Liang-shu-he (梁叔纥). Here Pound mistaked "hillock" (丘) as the father's given name, which is actually the son's. Later in the same canto, Pound retold the father's brave behavior in detail: "when he was attacking a city / his men had passed under the drop gate / And the warders then dropped it, so Hillock caught / the whole weight on his shoulder, and held till his / last man had got out." (Canto VIII 274) "His second son was Kung-fu-tseu" who was poor but worked hard enough to get respected and married Pien (Kung's wife, "Pien-kuan-chi" 亓官氏). Kung was the "supervisor of cattle" and the "inspector of Markets". These lines record Confucius's early poor life (before the age of 20). Nevertheless, in the middle of the quotations stand out two lines:

> Taught and the not taught. Kung and Eleusis
> to catechumen alone (Canto LIII 272)

"Kung and Eleusis" occur not for the first time. In Canto VII (258), Pound capitalized the two proper nouns: "Between KUNG and ELEUSIS". "The phrase 'Between Kung

① It's the author of the book who highlighted the different names of Confucius in bold type.

and Eleusis' names the two most important poles between which human value systems must be established: 'the ethical life and the sacred mysteries'." (Terrell, 1993: 210) It's a key phrase in the universe of *The Cantos*, presenting "one of creative tension between the rational civic order of Confucius and the mysteries of ancient Greek religion" (Cookson, 2001: 74). The proper nouns — Kung, Kungfutseu, Confucius, Chung Ni 仲尼 have become symbols of an orderly civilized world.

Surely, Kung walks peacefully into the cantos, and since then he speaks, acts and comments along to the very end of the epic. Pound made Confucius alive in his cantos, as a teacher, as an educator, as an Emperor (Canto LVII 312) and a law-maker. Sometimes Confucius speaks in Chinese and is juxtaposed with Yao (尧), Shun (舜), and Yu (禹):

> Chose learning from Yao, Shun and Kungfutseu,
> from Yu leader of waters. (Canto LVIII 320)

Sometimes he speaks in English, and stands side by side with Western philosophers, jurists or scientists:

> Agassiz, Kung, to avoid the encirclement (Canto C 736)

> in Kung, in Ocellus, Coke, Agassiz (Canto CVII 782)

Agassiz is Alexander Emanuel Agassiz (1835-1910), an American scientist born in Switzerland. "He is a Pound hero because of his close observation and accurate reporting." (Terrell, 1993: 562) Ocellus (or Occelus) is a 5th-century-BC Pythagorean philosopher, and Pound associated him with the important philosophers of light, and attributes to him the phrase "to build light" (Canto XCIV 662) (Terrell, 1993: 492). Coke is Sir Edward Coke, an English jurist who fought for justice against James I and Charles I (Terrell, 1993: 585). Pound put Kung, Ocellus, Coke and Agassiz in the same poetic line, intending to say that Kung, who's concerned with moral science, is a perfect man of philosopher, jurist and scientist.

Pound admired Confucius, "honouring Kung with the rites" (Canto LVI 306). He agreed with Yong Tching (Yong Zheng 雍正) who "putt out Xtianity" (means "put out Christianity") and reckoned "Xtians being such sliders and liars" (Canto LXI 334). For Christians are disturbers and destroyers of Kung's orderly civilized world:

Xtians are disturbing good customs
seeking to uproot Kung's law
seeking to break up Kung's teaching. (Canto LXI 334)

"Good customs" are highly advocated in a civilized society. Kung's law and teaching make an orderly world come true. However, Christians, as for Pound and Yong Zheng, are intruders who seek to destroy it.

The doctrines of Confucius have shaped Pound's ideas on economics and politics. Pound is a supporter of Mencius's ideas on distribution, and he hates unfair or false distributions of officials or governments. He recorded in Canto LXI:

Officers at Tientsing
who faked rice distribution
and gave bad rice to the needy
can damn well pay up what they have embezzled. (Canto LXI 334-345)

"Officers at Tientsing" lack the basic personality — honesty (*cheng* 诚). Pound sustained "that treasure of honesty" is "the treasure of states" (Canto LXXVII 490). And for Pound, Confucius never cheats:

From Kung's porch, 門 mên^3,
and not cheat the Administration. (Canto XCVIII 711)

States, which have lost the law of Chung Ni, are doomed to fall, such as the Mongolian Yuan Dynasty (Pound's Mongols):

Mongols are fallen
from losing the law of Chung Ni
(Confucius) 仲 (Canto LVI 308)
尼

"Chung Ni" and "Confucius" stand side by side with the Chinese characters "仲尼", which shows Pound's strong affirmation of Confucius's doctrines. "Kung" or any other forms of Confucius's name could almost symbolize an orderly and harmonious society in *The Cantos*.

Pound's Chinese translations should not be ignored though it's been a controversial topic since they came out. Pound is a language genius. He translated from Chinese, Anglo-Saxon, French, Greek, Hindi, Italian, Japanese and Latin. Among Pound's abundant achievements in translations, his Chinese translations are outstanding. He started his Chinese translations with ancient poems, which resulted in the well-known *Cathay* in the early 1910s when he had no idea about Chinese characters. He later translated three of the "Four Books" — *Da Xue*, *Zhong Yong*, *Lun Yu* and the Chinese anthology *Shi Jing*. His Chinese translations are as much censured as praised. Some scholars blamed him for misinterpreting Confucianism and taking advantage of Chinese culture. Some scholars maintained that Pound appropriated Chinese culture in order to save the disordered Western world. Some scholars stood in the middle and tried to give an objective comment:

> A great many things — positive and negative — can be said of Pound's Chinese translation, and indeed, much has been written on this inexhaustible topic. To say the least, Pound's achievement in Chinese translation is a mixed blessing. Whether it is awkward, inaccurate, unfaithful, distorted, half-understood, or misunderstood, almost all critics and scholars agree that Pound is above all inventive, a view represented by Hugh Kenner in his "The Invention of China," which in turn echoes T. S. Eliot's famous statement that Pound "invented" China.[①]

The author agrees with the latter two standpoints. Pound's Chinese translations should not be judged from the traditional criteria of translation because he has created while translating. It could be called "creative translation". When we consider his translations, we should not forget that he is also a poet, a great modernist poet. Pound's Confucian translations are concise and poetic. Readers could see "the possibilities of speed and brevity" (Kenner, 1988: 18). As a matter of fact, Pound aimed at saving the chaotic West with his creative Chinese translations, and some errors or mistakes were probably deliberately made by Mr. Pound. Readers need to recognize the nature of Pound's unconventional practice as a poet-translator.

Cultural salvation is the ultimate purpose of Pound's poetic revolution and translations. Pound is a poet who lived in the past. But he's always made efforts to "make it new". He "sought to launch a movement of 'American Renaissance' through

---

① Huang, G. Y. 2005. Chinese translations. In D. P. Tryphonopoulosand and S. J. Adams (Eds.), *The Ezra Pound Encyclopedia* (pp. 59-61). Westport & London: Greenwood Press.

cultural interference" (王庆, 董洪川, 2018: 97). Pound's ideas on cultural salvation originated from his discontent with the realities of the USA when he started his career as a young man. Pound's brief professional career at Crawfordsville was ended because he offered a homeless thespian shelter for a night (Stock, 2011: 41). The accident gave him a chance to leave Crawfordsville to Venice. He had a "crying need" for civilization (Stock, 2011: 40). He's sought great civilizations around the world. In the years of 1911 and 1912, he published a series of articles — "I gather the limbs of Osiris" in *The New Age*. Osiris, a god in Egyptian mythology, is connected with fertility. He is known for his story of his death at the hands of his brother Seth and his subsequent restoration to a new life as the ruler of the afterlife.[①] It's said that Seth murdered him, cut his body into pieces, and scattered them in different places. It's his wife Isis who gathered the pieces of his body, but not all, and finally restored him a new life. Therefore, Osiris is a metaphor. It figuratively refers to excellent cultures scattered around the world. Pound was determined to do the job of Isis — to gather the magnificent cultures all over the world so as to bring them into a new life. And the resurgence of new cultures could save the shattered world. Both his numerous translations and encyclopedic *Cantos* show his diligent and persistent efforts in carrying out cultural salvation. Among them all, his Confucian translations and his frequent references to Confucius in *The Cantos* convince us that Confucianism is the best antidote to the chaotic West.

7.2 Confucian Scholarship

However, in the field of Confucian studies, Pound's Confucianism doesn't get enough attention from Confucian scholars. Lan (2005: 8-9) argued: "In American academia, although Confucian experts are not unaware of Pound's Confucian translations, few have taken seriously his commitment to modernizing Confucianism in Western contexts." Pound's Confucian translations have received limited attention in Confucian scholarship. According to Lan (2005: 9), "Wing-tsit Chan is the only major Confucian scholar to have written a short review of Pound's translations". A newly published American critical archive *Ezra Pound: The Contemporary Reviews* (Erkkila, 2011) serves as an encyclopedic book to get to know Pound's publications, but it is distressing to find that no single review is on Pound's Confucian translations.

① From *Youdao* digital dictionary — *The New Oxford American Dictionary.*

Luckily in the checklist of additional reviews, the author found a piece "Ezra Pound's translation of Confucian analects reprinted".① But only a title, anonymously and insufficiently, stands there.

Wing-tsit Chan (1954: 371) considered that "this volume is an excellent job of book-making, a great attraction is its reproduction of the ninth-century stone-inscriptions of the classics".② On the one hand, Chan complimented Pound on his "beautiful English and poetic insight"; on the other hand, Chan criticized his ideographic interest, which has "led him astray" and "made his version unnecessarily complicated" (Chan, 1954: 372). de Bary (1996: xii) has noticed his contribution to Confucianism. He wrote in the preface to his book *The Trouble with Confucianism* that Ezra Pound "saw Confucius as the quintessential Chinese sage" and was "among those who appreciated Confucius's teaching as virtually ageless". In America today, Weiming Tu (1989: 132), the leading New Confucian, showed his respect for Pound in a brief note — he's amazed by the "fascinating" and "insightful observations" in Pound's versions.

Besides these comments, what also deserves mention is Pound's contact with a modern Confucian, Carsun Chang. Chang visited Pound many times from November 1953 to May 1955 when Pound was confined in St. Elizabeths Hospital. Chang marveled at "the 'remarkable genius' of Pound's translations of many paragraphs in *The Analects*, but he felt that sometimes Pound 'went too far'". Chang even asked Pound to write an introduction for his book on Neo-Confucian philosophy. Pound wrote one page, but Chang decided not to use it because Pound had written the introduction "like a poet" rather than a scholar.③ Even so, Chang paid his respect to Pound sincerely in a 30 March 1957 letter to Pound: "The Chinese own you a great deal for spreading Confucian ideas."④

As for Pound's influence on American Confucian scholars, it's hard to trace the relationship between Pound's Confucianism and their studies. But some scholars, such as Theodore de Bary and Weiming Tu, might have been influenced to some degree by Pound's Confucian translations and his ideas. Though it's hard to trace their intersections, some similarities of their Confucian thoughts are apparent. For instance, as for the

① The article "Ezra Pound's translation of Confucian analects reprinted" was originally published by *San Francisco Chinese World* on 21 January 1954.

② Wing-tsit Chan, well known as 陈荣捷 in China, is a famous Chinese American Confucian scholar. Pound's translation arouse his attention and he wrote a review shortly after Pound's publication of *Confucius: The Great Digest and The Unwobbiling Pivot* and published it in *Philosophy East and West* (Chan, 1954: 371-373).

③ See William Maughton's memoir in Qian (2008: 105-106).

④ Consult the letter in Qian (2008: 103).

virtues of the gentleman / noble man in *The Analects*, de Bary (1996: 36) argued:

> ...if humaneness (*jen*) riteness (*li*) are the two most prominent virtues of the gentleman / noble man in the *Analects*, learning (*hsüeh* 学) and knowledge together constitute a third subject of comparable importance.

It happens that Pound also considered learning (学) and knowledge as an inevitable method to become a whole man, and a whole man must possess the virtue *li* 礼 and finally reach *ren* 仁. As for the role of actions, de Bary (1996: 42) maintained: "Confucian gentlemen accepted this present world as the one in which the Way was to be realized, by actions that would also transform it." Pound also attached great importance to "action". He insisted on "the 'know thyself' carried into action" (*Con* 21) and prefers to "clarify the intelligence in straight action" (*Con* 36).

Weiming Tu and Pound shared a similar attitude toward man — the human being. For Weiming Tu, man is not only the created but also the creator. For Pound, "man is a maker: not as one making up some order of his own, but as the agent of the self-ordering energies of the Cosmos" (Qtd. in Moody, 1982: 135-136).

7.3 Amateur Readers

Pound's Confucian translations have reached all libraries at major American universities. And Pound's Confucian "Four Books" is considered as influential as James Legge's and other prominent Confucian scholars' versions.[①] Lan (2005: 9) remarked like this:

> In the twentieth century few have done more than Pound to bring Confucius to English readers. His rendering of the first three of the Confucian Four Books remains one of the major Confucian translations in English available in university libraries all over America and consistently attracts readers. While there are other English translations of Confucius that are considered more accurate than Pound's, many ordinary readers still find Pound's translation more readable and memorable.

An Amazon customer left such comments after his purchase:

① The author visited the library of California State University, Los Angeles, during his stay in USA as a visiting scholar and he found such arrangement.

> My own copy of Pound's "Confucius" was purchased many years ago. It's very well-thumbed and heavily annotated, and I often return to it. I've also studied Arthur Waley's more exact translation carefully, and a few others. But the Confucian lines that stick in my mind always seem to be those of Pound.①

He honestly shared his reading experience and looked on Pound's Confucian translations as something memorable. He must be a learned and sensitive reader for he's also given his suggestions to ordinary readers:

> My advice would be to ignore the gripers, most of whom don't have direct access to the Chinese text anyway, and to read Pound's version of Confucius. He was a literary genius and got it right most of the time, and you'd learn a great deal from it. Pound's "Confucius" has always found and will continue to find readers. I think it's because, as Confucius says: "Those who know aren't up to those who love..."②

There are some misreadings and misinterpretations in Pound's Confucius works, but Pound has articulated the core of Confucianism in his translations and poetic writing. Enjoy reading Pound's Confucius, take the advice of the Amazon commentator and "ignore the gripers".

"Pound and Confucianism" is a complex research topic because of Pound's ardent involvement with Confucianism for over half a century. The span of time is even a bit longer than the creation of his epic *The Cantos*.③ However, the studies of Pound and Confucianism didn't reach China until the 1980s, so the studies of Pound and Confucianism in China started much later than those in the West. Comparatively speaking, Pound's poetry, especially his poetic revolution, namely Imagism, was introduced to China much earlier, in the 1920s.④ Pound's acceptance and assimilation of Chinese culture, such as, simply speaking, Chinese poetry, Chinese characters and Confucianism, have been widely explored in the past decades.

Pound regarded Confucianism as an antidote to the sordid mundane reality that had come to characterize the modern world. He believed that "Kung's life appears to

---

① See https://www.amazon.com/Confucius-great-digest-Unwobbling-pivot/product-reviews/B0007DUWVW/ref=cm_cr_dp_d_show_all_btm?ie=UTF8&reviewerType=all_reviews.

② See https://www.amazon.com/Confucius-great-digest-Unwobbling-pivot/product-reviews/B0007DUWVW/ref=cm_cr_dp_d_show_all_btm?ie=UTF8&reviewerType=all_reviews.

③ According to Achilles Fang, the very first lines of *The Cantos* were published in 1917 (2016: I-7). But Pound started to know and read Confucius in 1908 and his attachment to Confucianism lasted the rest of his life.

④ It was Yanling Liu (刘延陵) who firstly introduced Ezra Pound into China in 1922 (蒋洪新, 2014: 366).

be in conformity with the best modern views" (*GK* 272). Although he "wanted Confucianism as Confucius had it" (*EPCF* 105), he actually tried to modernize Confucius's doctrines to meet the needs of the modern West. Pound's Confucianism can be categorized into three perspectives: Pound's ethics on man and self — self-civilization; Pound's ethics on man and society; Pound's ethics on man and nature.

Pound's Confucianism starts from "to know thyself" (知人), which he emphasized three times in his work *Guide to Kulchur*. He insisted on "the 'know thyself' carried into action. Said action also serves to clarify the self knowledge" (*Con* 21). One eventually becomes a real man who possesses *ren* 仁. Regarding the relationship between man and society, the family is the basic cell of society. "敬 reverence / order 孝 / 'Parents naturally hope their sons will be gentlemen.'" (Canto XCVIII 711) Through the voice of the poetic persona, Pound uttered his own expectations for "gentlemen". Such gentlemen establish the order in the society or keep the order in a sound way.

Modern China is peaceful and has been at peace with other countries for years. However, some problems have still inevitably occurred in the process of modernization. Some businessmen are driven by the need for profits and might probably lose their conscience. Pound attached great importance to *yi* 义 instead of *li* 利. In *The Cantos*, he quoted Mencius' words "why must say profit" (何必曰利) more than once. One quotation runs as follows:

> pu erh. "Why must say profit
>
> 利 (the grain cut). (Canto LXXXVII 595)

In these lines we can hear Pound rather than Mencius speaking about what a peaceful and harmonious society needs, even though "why must say profit" (何必曰利) in a quotation mark.

Ezra Pound and Confucius remain relevant for China. In the 21st Century, a peaceful and modern China still needs Confucius, for "Kung is to China as is water to fishes" (Canto LIV 285). Chairman Xi respects and advocates the traditional Chinese culture and especially Confucianism. He stressed the "Core Socialist Values":

> Core socialist values comprise a set of moral principles summarized by central authorities as prosperity, democracy, civility, harmony, freedom, equality, justice, the rule of law, patriotism, dedication, integrity and friendship. ①

"This doctrine has been encouraged by the Communist Party of China (CPC) since its 18th Party Congress in late 2012. It has evolved into a national campaign to rebuild faith amid concerns that the world's second-largest economy has lost its moral compass during its three-decade economic miracle."② The "Core Socialist Values" actually contain three levels of meaning. At the national level, prosperity, democracy, civility and harmony consist of values our country aims for; at the level of society, freedom, equality, justice and the rule of law consist of values we tend towards; at the individual level, patriotism, dedication, integrity and friendship consist of values the individuals should embrace. Pound's ethics on man and nature, on man and society, and on man and self are in agreement with the three levels of "Core Socialist Values" (谭小翠, 2015: 29). Isn't this a coincidence?

Modern China needs modernized Confucianism. Today, China is one of the most prosperous nations in the world, but it's still undergoing modernization. Lai Chen (陈来, 2011: 28) stated that the redevelopment of Confucianism must be realized once China accomplishes modernization, and he further asserted that modernization is a priority in the resurrection of traditional thoughts. Modern China needs Confucianism, which can serve China well only when it is modernized. Although Pound "wanted Confucianism as Confucius had it", he unconsciously modernized Confucius when he translated the Confucian classics, paraphrased Confucian doctrines, interpreted Chinese ideograms, and wrote comments on Confucianism. We must never forget Pound's slogan — "Make it new!"

Every citizen needs to put forth the effort to enrich China both materially and spiritually. Liang (梁漱溟, 2017: 200) once made a daring prediction for the future of Western and Eastern cultures — Western culture will vary in the future while Eastern culture will be resurrected. This resurrected culture requires every Chinese citizen to work hard. Ordinary citizens and government officials must work hard together to create a beautiful and harmonious tomorrow. Pound wrote:

---

① From the news "Xi stresses core socialist values". 2014-2-26. http://en.people.cn/90785/8546696.html [2019-12-20].

② From the news "Xi stresses core socialist values". 2014-2-26. http://en.people.cn/90785/8546696.html [2019-12-20].

Sage men have plans,
simplicity a thousand generations, no man can change.
The Sage Emperor's heart is our heart,
His government is our government
yao² high, hsiao³ dawn
The Venerated Emperor
watched things grow with affection.
(Canto XCIX 715)

Although Pound did not realize the limits of Confucianism that the New Confucians have identified, his efforts to modernize Confucianism in the modern West should not be overlooked.

Conclusions

— Reconsidering Pound's Confucianism in the 21st Century

In the Confucian canto — Canto XIII was written four years after World War I — Pound wrote close to the end of the poem:

> And Kung said: "Wang ruled with moderation,
> In his day the State was well kept,
> And even I can remember
> A day when the historians left blanks in their writings,
> I mean, for things they didn't know,
> But that time seems to be passing." (Canto XIII 60)

It's Pound's opinion that is appearing through the voice of Kung although these lines are articulated by Kung. Pound narrated anecdotes of the past to make observations and conclusions about the present. "A day" seems to have gone when the state is well governed, and historians are honest or sincere enough to leave blanks for "things they didn't know". It may in fact be an allusion to Confucius's lament — *li beng yue huai* 礼崩乐坏 (the Confucian *li* has been badly destroyed and the state is in disorder). The allusion may include the post-World War II world in which Pound lived. In 1945, a few months after World War II, Pound quoted Tami Kume's remark at the end of his retranslation of *Da Xue*: "We are at the crisis point of the world." (*Con* 89) The lament is elevated to an urgent admonition. Living through the devastating turmoil of two world wars, Pound has the experience to make such observations. "The crisis point of the world" that Pound referred to may be a historical crossroad. Pound was asking what direction the world would take at this crucial moment in history. Pound, as a pioneering poet, was in tune with the modern world and anxious about its fate. Pound considered Confucianism the best antidote to the crisis he saw facing the West, so invoked an "immediate need of Confucius" even as early as the 1930s.

Framing Pound's Confucianism in this sense gives added significance to his

Confucian study. There are good reasons to conclude that Pound was neither retranslating and reinterpreting Confucian classics nor merely curious about them. He wasn't trying to impress readers with his knowledge of Chinese philosophy or trying to enrich his own writing with exotic Eastern allusions. Instead, Pound believed that the West needed Confucianism — a modernized Confucianism. Mencius complimented: "*Kong Zi, sheng ren zhi shi zhe ye* 孔子，圣人之时者也 (Confucius, the sage of the time)." Pound is also very complimentary: "Kung's life appears to be in conformity with the best modern views" and he "suspect[s] a minority has always held these views" (*GK* 272). Pound, to some degree, is a sage of the time because he committed himself to Confucianism when it was not popular to do so in the East and the West. Since the Western world, in Pound's view, had degenerated into a decayed and morally-absent desert, where human beings were separated and alienated from the self, society and nature. And Pound believed that Christianity was chiefly responsible for this miserable situation. Pound's critique of the problematic position of Christianity shows his sharp perception of modern society. He moved Confucian ideas into a new organic whole. His Confucianism is centered on the self, society and nature.

Pound's Confucianism records a man's growing-up process, like an acorn growing into an oak tree. A man begins his moral development at the moment of *zhi ren* 知人 (knowing men), which means knowing others, knowing self and knowing human nature. Among the three possible meanings, the last is the most important one. In his understanding of Confucianism, human nature is innately good, an idea Pound had inherited from Mencius's view of human nature — *si duan* 四端, among which *ren* 仁 is the core. In the process of achieving *ren* 仁, *cheng* 诚 is pivotal. Once the personal order is established, man moves to familial and social developments. *Xiao ti* 孝悌 is crucial to establishing a sound familial order and *ti* 悌 is especially effective for establishing a harmonious social order. What's more, the Confucian doctrines *zheng ming* 正名, *li* 礼 and *yi* 义（義）play indispensable roles in creating social harmony.

What Pound found particularly attractive in Confucianism was that "the school of Kung included intelligence without cutting it from its base [nature]" (*SP* 86). Pound's concept of nature originates from Chinese *Tian* 天 (heaven) and is based on *Li yi fen shu* 理一分殊. He interpreted heaven as nature. Pound's nature has a broader implication and it consists of heaven and earth. Since absolute sincerity raises man up to be the third partner of heaven and earth, the relationship between man and nature is the partnership rather than the ruler and his dominion. To put it in other words, man is a part of organic nature, and nature is also embedded in man. Pound believed that transcendental and supernatural power (which is *tian ming* 天命) exists in the universe, and the universe, as an organic whole, operates according to natural law, which is *Li* 理 or *Tao* 道. Pound's ethics on man and nature is well manifested in his interpretation of *Tao* 道 and the unity of the way of heaven and the way of man. In this process, *cheng* 诚 is also important. Pound's Confucianism could be illustrated in the following diagram.

The wholeness of Pound's Confucian philosophy is as shown in Figure 1. The concentric circles represent the cosmos. The shadowy part is *yin* 阴 and the other part is *yang* 阳. All things created by heaven are the combinations of *yin* and *yang*, including human beings. As early as in 1910 in *The Spirit of Romance*, Pound recognized that "the little cosmos 'corresponds' to the greater, that man has in him both 'sun' and 'moon'" (*SR* 94). In the universe, *yin* and *yang* move interactively like the sun and the moon moving to offer day and night to the earth. The order of cosmos (the law of nature or the ultimate principle 天理) is revealed by *yuan heng li zhen* 元亨利贞, representing the four seasons respectively: spring, summer, autumn and winter. In Chinese philosophy, "元亨利贞" are the four virtues of the universe. Take the growing-up process of a plant as an example. It sprouts in spring, blooms in summer, grows fruits in autumn, and matures in winter. The four seasons go in turn and all things are generated; therefore "元亨利贞" is a representative example of *tian li* 天理. In Confucianism, the four virtues of the universe (元亨利贞) correspond respectively to the four virtues of human beings — *ren* 仁, *li* 礼, *yi* 义, *zhi* 智.

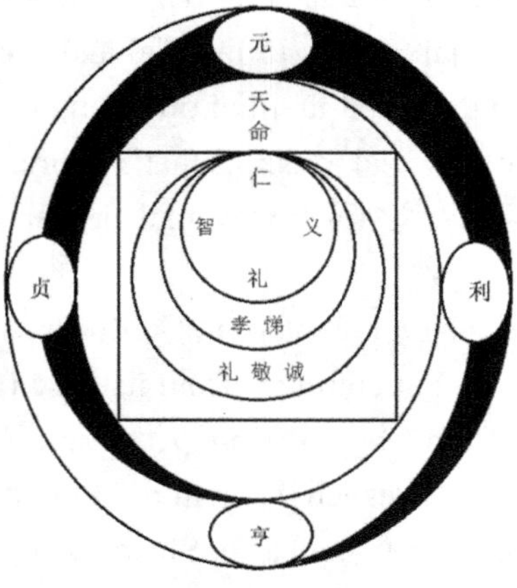

Figure 1　Ezra Pound's Confucianism

The square in the concentric circles refers to the earth under heaven. Man, as the most salient creature, lives on the earth. According to Mencius, man is born with a good nature — "仁义礼智". The elite who is able to receive *tian ming* 天命 (the mandate of heaven) is *wang* 王 (king). As discussed in Chapter 3, Wu Wang 武王 complied with the mandate of heaven to overthrow the regime of the despot Zhou Wang 纣王 so as to liberate people from oppression. Shun 舜 and other Chinese emperors who also received *tian ming* led the states to prosperity. Otherwise, a dynasty was doomed to perish. *Tian ming* contains the good virtues of man. Namely, the man who receives *tian ming* must be a person possessing *ren* 仁, which is the key to *si duan*.

The three circles in the square reflect Pound's ideas on the socially moral development of man. The inner circle in the square represents an individual self who establishes the personal order through self-cultivation. A man with the personal order is a man with the virtues of "仁义礼智". Once the personal order is established, it naturally moves to the building of the familial order and thus the constructing of social harmony. In this process, *xiao ti* 孝悌 is essential, especially for building the familial order. Pound wrote at the beginning of *The Pisan Cantos*: "Filial, fraternal affection is the root of humaneness / the root of the process." (Canto LXXIV 457) *Li* 礼, as one of *si duan*, manifests a good virtue of man, and at the same time, it contributes to social harmony. Pound contended: "Peace comes of good manner." (Canto XCIX 718) *Cheng* 诚 and *jing* 敬 are not only crucial for self-cultivation but also indispensable for establishing a harmonious social order, and universal harmony between man and nature.

Pound's Confucianism has the following characteristics. First, Pound expanded Confucius's special concern for humanity to a larger degree. In his words, "man, man, man, humanity all over the page, land, and trees" (*SP* 94). Second, Pound particularly stressed Confucianism as a totalitarian philosophy running counter to Western philosophy. In accordance with the totalitarian philosophy, he contended that the universe is an organic whole. At the same time, his Confucianism, as a totalitarian philosophy, is characterized by inclusiveness. For instance, the unity of Confucianism and the Western Neo-Platonic philosophy of light is his own construction so as to make Confucianism easily accessible to Western readers. Third, he made Confucian metaphysics less mysterious. The Confucian *Tao* 道 is the process or ethics which accesses to every person. William Cookson (2001: 18) commented in the introduction to *Selected Prose, 1909-1965*: "When Pound's errors have been forgotten, the humanity and inclusiveness of his concern will be remembered."

What's more, Pound contributed to Confucian scholarship. For Pound, the Western world was undergoing a special period of *li beng yue huai* 礼崩乐坏. In order to turn the chaotic West into a society with *li yue ren he* 礼乐仁和, Pound committed himself to carrying forward the tradition of Confucianism. At the end of Canto XIII, Pound expressed his self-ordained mission: "The blossoms of the apricot / Blow from the east to the west, / And I have tried to keep them from falling." (Canto XIII 60) It's said that Confucius usually taught in a pavilion near a big apricot tree in his hometown Qufu 曲阜. So "the blossoms of apricot" is an emblem of Confucius's teachings. It shows Pound's determination to be a liberal Confucian disciple and to maintain and spread the Confucian doctrines worldwide. Pound has "tried to write Paradise" where man and nature co-exist in a perfect harmony (Notes for CXVII 822). However, close to the end of *The Cantos*, Pound deplored:

> That I lost my center
>   fighting the world.
> The dreams clash
>   and are shattered —
> and that I tried to make a paradiso
>   terrestre. (Canto CXVII 822)

With deep regret and disappointment, Pound wrote down such a verse. He must have felt lonely when fighting against the world during the time when Confucianism was not favorable in both China and the West. This loneliness may result from the cruel fact that "the European mind stops" (Canto CXV 814). Coincidentally, Pound's lament accords with Confucius's lament at the beginning of the movie *Kong Zi* (《孔子》) directed by Mei Hu (胡玫) in 2010:

> 衰老了，很久没有梦见周公了，礼乐仁和的梦想，只能托付给未来了。
> I've grown old. It's so long since I last dreamed of the Duke of Zhou. My ideals of ethics, music, humanity and harmony can be fulfilled only in times to come...①

Pound's lament shows his awareness of the difficulty in implementing Confucianism in the West. His appeal for "immediate need of Confucius" in 1937 had not stopped

① It is from the bilingual subtitles of the movie.

World War II, and his enthusiastic translation of the Confucian classics and frequently-quoted Confucian terms in the later cantos might not make the Cold War cool down. In this case, some critics may conclude that Pound has made a futile effort. However, his transmission of Confucianism, especially when Confucianism was under unfavorable situations in the East and West, has contributed a lot to the maintenance and development of Confucianism although misinterpretations existed deliberately or unintentionally.

Pound's Confucianism has been dealt with extensively by both Occidental and Oriental scholars. It has won him not only fame but also doubts because some scholars criticized Pound for what they believed was his taking advantage of Chinese culture. Regardless, Pound's involvement with Confucianism deserves repeated exploration, in different eras and at different sites. Just as Torrey (1999: 126) declared: "To be praised was desirable, to be criticized acceptable, but to be forgotten was death." Pound has never been forgotten. The study of Ezra Pound is increasing during the 21st century, especially in China. Along with the flourishing study of Pound's Confucianism, Pound's close contact with other Chinese "religions", which was first noticed by Western scholars①, has also started to receive attention by Chinese scholars. Of course, the Confucianism of Ezra Pound sometimes is notoriously related to Fascism and Anti-Semitism, a concern that has been explored by scholars, such as Tim Redman, Serenella Zanotti (2010) and Alex Houen (2010). However, the time has proved that Pound, a modern poet living during a period of turmoil, held high ideals and lofty aspirations in his attempt to assist his generation in his "quest for Confucian ideals"(Sun, 2003). As a Chinese scholar who knows Confucianism, the author understands Pound's good intentions in transmitting Confucian thoughts. His life-long commitment to Confucianism rests on his strong belief that Confucius could offer a better anschauung for human beings, and Confucianism is the best medicine for the Western ailments. This is a task undertaken by contemporary New Confucianism, especially the third generation of New Confucians represented by Weiming Tu. In this sense, no matter how misinterpreted or mishandled Pound's Confucian texts might be, his attempt to transmit Confucianism from the East to the West will prove to be increasingly meaningful.

---

① For example, David Hsin-Fu Wand discussed Pound through his embrace of Kuanon (观音, the goddess revered both by Taoists and Buddhists), and has joined the company of Wang Wei and Su Shi in this syncretic tradition. See "To the summit of Tai Shan: Ezra Pound's use of Chinese mythology" (Wand, 1974: 3-12).

Glossary

Column I provides the *Hanyu pinyin* of Chinese characters that appear in the book. Column II offers the Chinese characters both in simplified and complicated forms if the latter form appears in the book. Column III gives the transliteration of the Chinese characters used by Pound or other scholars.

I *Hanyu pinyin*	**II Chinese characters**	**III Transliteration**
ben	本	Pen
ben ye	本业/本業	pen yeh
cheng	诚	Ch'eng
Cheng Tang	成汤	Tching
Da Xue	《大学》	*Ta Hio*, *The Great Learning*, *The Great Digest*
Dao	道	Tao
dao shi	道士	Taosers
fa	发/發	
Gao Tao	皋陶	Kao Yao
Gu Hongming	辜鸿铭	Ku Hweng-Ming
he bi yue li	何必曰利	ho^{2} pi$^{4\text{-}5}$ yüeh$^{4\text{-}5}$ li^{4}
Kang Xi	康熙	Kang Hi
Kong Zi	孔子	Confucius, Kung-Fu-Tse, K'ung the Master, K'ung fu Tsze, Kung-tze, Kung
	孔孟（的）	Confucio-Mencian
li xing jin hu ren	力行近乎仁	li^{4} hsing^{2} chin^{4} hu^{1} jên^{2}
Liang Hui Wang	梁惠王	King Hwuy of Leang
ling	灵/靈	Ling^{2}
Liu Dianjue	刘殿爵	D. C. Lau
Lun Yu	《论语》	*The Analects*
Meng Zi	《孟子》	
Meng Zi	孟子	Mencius, Mang Tse, Mang Tsze

Continued

I *Hanyu pinyin*	II Chinese characters	III Transliteration
ren	仁	Jen
ren zhi yi li	仁智义礼	Jen^2 chih^4 i-li / jen chih i-li
ri ri xin	日日新	jih^4 jih^4 hsin^1
si duan	四端	four beginnings
ti	悌	t'i
Wu Wang	武王	King Wu
xian	显/顯	hsien
xiao	孝	Hsiao
xin	新	hsin^1
xin shu huai	心术坏	hsin^1 shu$^{4-5}$ hai^{4}"
xue	学/學	
yi qi	义气/義氣	i^4 Ch'i^4
yi ren	一人	i jin
Yao	尧	Yaou
Yuan Rang	原壤	Yuan Jang
Ye Gong	叶公	The Duke of Sheh
Dian	曾点	Si-hoa or Chieh
Junmai Zhang	张君劢	Carson Chang
zhen	震	chên
zheng ming	正名	Ch'ing Ming, Cheng Ming
zhong	衷	chung$^{1-4}$
Zhong Yong	《中庸》	*The Doctrine of the Mean, The Unwobbling Pivot*
zhong yong zhi dao	中庸之道	Ts'ung yung ching tao
Dunyi Zhou	周敦颐	Tcheou Tun-y
Zi Gong	子贡	Tze-Kung
Zi Lu	子路	Tze-yu
Zi Xia	子夏	Tse-Hsia

References

常沛文. 1986. 艾兹拉·庞德传播中国文化的使者. 外国文学, (5): 91-93.

陈来. 2011. 传统与现代——人文主义的视界. 北京: 读书·生活·新知三联书店.

杜维明. 2012. 体知儒学——儒家当代价值的九次对话. 杭州: 浙江大学出版社.

胡平. 2013. 论庞德《比萨诗章》中诗化的儒家思想. 中国比较文学, (4): 125-132.

胡平. 2015. 投射与融通: 庞德《比萨诗章》中的新柏拉图主义与儒家思想. 外国语文研究, (6): 2-9.

胡平. 2017. 庞德《比萨诗章》研究. 上海: 上海大学出版社.

蒋洪新. 2001. 庞德的翻译理论研究. 外国语, (4): 77-80.

蒋洪新. 2006. 庞德的《七湖诗章》与潇湘八景. 外国文学评论, (3): 31-37.

蒋洪新. 2014. 庞德研究. 上海: 上海外语教育出版社.

蒋洪新, 李春长. 2014. 庞德研究文集. 南京: 译林出版社.

蓝峰. 1984. “维护说”析——庞德诗歌理论及其与孔子思想的关系. 文艺研究, (4): 115-122.

老子. 2011. 老子道德经注. [魏]王弼注. 楼宇烈校释. 北京: 中华书局.

李正栓, 孙蔚. 2011. 庞德对中国诗歌与思想的借鉴. 当代外国文学, (1): 65-71.

梁漱溟. 2017. 东西文化及其哲学. 2 版. 上海: 上海人民出版社.

刘心莲. 2001. 理解抑或误解? ——美国诗人庞德与中国之关系的重新思考. 外国文学, (6): 73-78.

冒键. 2001. 踩高跷的“孔子”: 庞德与中国古典文化. 当代外国文学, (2): 82-90.

欧荣. 2013a. “王, 秉承鸿业”——论庞德在《御座诗章》中的“以讹传讹”. 外国文学评论, (4): 72-85.

欧荣. 2013b. 说不尽的《七湖诗章》和“艺格符换”. 英美文学研究论丛, (1): 229-249.

钱兆明. 2015. 中华才俊与庞德. 北京: 中央编译出版社.

宋晓春. 2014. 新柏拉图之光与庞德的《中庸》翻译. 中国比较文学, (2): 127-137.

孙宏. 1999. 论庞德的史诗与儒家经典. 外国文学评论, (2): 20-30.

孙宏. 2017. 从命名者到“一人大学”: 庞德的诗学话语探踪. 外国文学, (2): 23-33.

索金梅. 2003. 庞德《诗章》中的儒学. 天津: 南开大学出版社.

谭小翠. 2015a. 博中见微 开拓创新——评蒋洪新教授的新著《庞德研究》. 当代外国文学, (1): 154-159.

谭小翠. 2015b. 一以贯之——庞德与儒学的情缘. 宁波大学学报 (人文科学版), (3): 24-29.

陶乃侃. 2006. 庞德与中国文化. 北京: 首都师范大学出版社.

王贵明. 2001a. 《比萨诗章》中的儒家思想. 国外文学, (2): 87-95.

王贵明. 2001b. 汉字的魅力与《诗章》的精神. 北京理工大学学报 (社会科学版), (1): 36-41.

王贵明. 2003. 庞德之于中国文化功过论——与《理解抑或误解? ——美国诗人庞德与中国关系的重新思考》的作者商榷. 外国文学, (3): 100-106.

王辉. 2004. 理雅各、庞德《论语》译本比较. 四川外语学院学报, (5): 140-144.

王庆, 董洪川. 2018. 我曾试图建立一个人间乐园——埃兹拉·庞德与文化救赎. 外语教学, (1): 97-103.

王伟均, 陈义华. 2017. 庞德《诗章》中儒家文化的视觉化分析. 外国语文研究, (2): 26-38.

吴其尧. 2006. 庞德与中国文化: 兼论外国文学在中国文化现代化中的作用. 上海: 上海外语教育出版社.

杨平. 2010. 创造性翻译与文化挪用——庞德的儒经译介评析. 天津外国语学院学报, (1): 30-36.

杨平. 2011. 中西文化交流视域下的《论语》英译研究. 北京: 光明日报出版社.

叶维廉. 2008. 庞德与潇湘八景. 台北: 台湾大学出版中心.

赵毅衡. 1996. 儒者庞德——后期《诗章》中的中国. 中国比较文学, (1): 42-60.

赵毅衡. 2003. 诗神远游——中国如何改变了美国现代诗. 上海: 上海译文出版社.

周建新. 2011. 庞德翻译观探析. 东北师范大学学报 (哲学社会科学版), (4): 153-156.

朱熹. 2011. 四书章句集注. 北京: 中华书局.

朱伊革. 2007. 林纾与庞德误读和误译的解构主义理据. 上海师范大学学报 (哲学社会科学版), (6): 126-130.

朱伊革. 2012. 庞德诗学及其《诗章》的孔子思想渊源与呈现. 上海师范大学学报 (哲学社会科学版), (2): 110-117.

祝朝伟. 2006. 庞德与林舒的翻译. 淮海工学院学报 (社会科学版), (1): 69-72.

Albright, D. 2001. Early Cantos I-XLI. In I. B. Nadel (Ed.), *The Cambridge Companion to Ezra Pound* (pp. 59-91). Shanghai: Shanghai Foreign Language Education Press.

Ames, Roger T., and Henry Rosemont, Jr. (Trans.) 1998. *The Analects of Confucius: A Philosophical Translation.* New York: Ballantine Books.

Auchincloss, K. 1999. Fanfare for the common man. *Newsweek*, 134 (25): 48.

Barber, N. 2006. *The Complete Idiot Guide to European History*. New York: Penguin.

Bernstein, M. A. 1980. *The Tale of the Tribe: Ezra Pound and the Modern Verse Epic*. Princeton: Princeton University Press.

Bilenchi, R. 1979. Rapallo 1941. *Paideuma*, 8 (3): 431-442.

Brzezinski, Z. 1956. Totalitarianism and rationality. *The American Political Science Review*, 50 (3): 751-763.

Bush, R. Confucius erased: The missing ideograms in *The Pisan Cantos*. In Z. M. Qian (Ed.), *Ezra Pound and China* (pp. 163-192). Ann Arbor: University of Michigan Press.

Carpenter, H. 1988. *A Serious Character: The Life of Ezra Pound*. New York: Dell Publishing.

Cayley, J. 1984. Ch'eng, or sincerity. *Paideuma*, 13 (2): 201-210.

Chan, W. 1954. Review of *Confucius: The Great Digest and The Unwobbiling Pivot* by Ezra Pound. *Philosophy East and West*, 3 (4): 371-373.

Chan, W. 1963. *A Source Book in Chinese Philosophy.* Princeton: Princeton University Press.

Chang, Y. 1988. Pound's Chinese translations. *Paideuma*, 17 (1): 113-132.

Cheadle, M. P. 1989. The vision of light in Ezra Pound's *The Unwobbling Pivot*. *Twentieth Century Literature*, 35 (2): 113-130.

Cheadle, M. P. 1997. *Ezra Pound's Confucian Translations*. Ann Arbor: University of Michigan Press.

Cookson, W. 2001. *A Guide to the Cantos of Ezra Pound*. New York: Persea Books.

Davie, D. 1982. *Ezra Pound*. Phoenix edn. Chicago and London: University of Chicago Press.

de Bary, W. T. 1996. *The Trouble with Confucianism*. Cambridge and London: Harvard University Press.

Dembo, L. S. 1963. *The Confucian Odes of Ezra Pound*. London: Faber & Faber.

Eastham, S. 2004. In Pound's China — the stone books speak. *Paideuma*, 33 (1): 89-117.

Erkkila, B. 2011. *Ezra Pound: The Contemporary Reviews* (American Critical Archives, Book 18). Cambridge: Cambridge University Press.

Fang, A. 2016. *Materials for the Study of Pound's Cantos*. Shanghai: Zhongxi Press.

Flory, W. S. 2003. Confucius against confusion: Ezra Pound and the Catholic chaplain at Pisa. In Z. M. Qian (Ed.), *Ezra Pound and China* (pp. 143-162). Ann Arbor: University of Michigan Press.

Froula, C. 1983. *A Guide to Ezra Pound's Selected Poems*. New York: New Directions.

Gordon. D. 1988. And Moore: Marianne on Ezra's Confucius. *Paideuma*, 18 (3): 149-150.

Hatlen, B. 1996. Pound and nature: A reading of canto XXIII. *Paideuma*, 25 (1&2): 161-188.

Hayes, C. J. H. 1938. The challenge of totalitarianism. *The Public Opinion Quarterly*, 2 (1): 21-26.

Heine, S. J. 2001. Self as cultural product: An examination of East Asian and North American selves. *Journal of Personality*, 69 (6): 881-905.

Hinchman, L. P. 1990. The idea of individuality: Origins, meaning, and political significance. *The Journal of Politics*, 52 (3): 759-781.

Houen, A. 2010. Anti-Semitism. In I. B. Nadel (Ed.), *Ezra Pound in Context* (pp. 391-401). Cambridge: Cambridge University Press.

Jackson, T. H. 1968. *The Early Poetry of Ezra Pound*. Cambridge: Harvard University Press.

Jin, S. P. 1994. Observation of natural scenes: Ta Hsüeh and Pound's later cantos. *Paideuma*, 23 (2&3): 7-44.

Kelley Jr., A. L. 1986. *Confucianism and the Meaning of The Cantos of Ezra Pound* (Unpublished doctoral dissertation). Indiana University, Bloomington.

Kenner, H. 1971. *The Pound Era*. 1st paper edn. Berkeley and Los Angeles: University of California Press.

Kenner, H. 1985. *The Poetry of Ezra Pound*. Lincoln and London: University of Nebraska Press. Kenner, H. 1988. Simplicities. In M. Smith and W. A. Ulmer (Eds.), *Ezra Pound: The Legacy of Kulchur* (pp. 11-24). Tuscaloosa and London: University of Alabama Press.

Kitayama, S., Markus, H. R., Matsumoto, H., et al. 1997. Individual and collective processes in the construction of the self: Self-enhancement in the United States and self-criticism in Japan. *Journal of Personality and Social Psychology*, 72 (6): 1245-1267.

Lan F. 2001. Ezra Pound's etymographic reading and his interpretation of Confucian texts. *Paideuma*, 30 (3): 23-38.

Lan, F. 2004. Ezra Pound/Ming Mao: A liberal disciple of Confucius. *Journal of Modern Literature*, 27 (1): 79-89.

Lan, F. 2005. *Ezra Pound' and Confucianism — Remaking Humanism in the Face of Modernity*. Toronto Buffalo London: University of Toronto Press.

Lau, D. C. (Trans.) 2008. *The Analects.* Chinese-English edn. Beijing: Zhonghua Book Company.

Lau, D. C. (Trans.) 2003. *Mencius*. Revised edn. London: Penguin Books.

Legge, J. (Trans.) 2009. *Confucius: Confucian Analects, The Great Learning and The Doctrine of the Mean*. New York: Dover Publications, Inc.

Li, Q. J. 2008. Ezra Pound's poetic mirror and the "China Cantos": The healing of the West. *Southeast Review of Asian Studies*, (30): 41-54.

Liebregts, P. 2004. *Ezra Pound and Neoplatonism*. Madison & Vancouver: Fairleigh Dickinson University Press.

Little, M. 1982. Pound's use of the word "totalitarian". *Paideuma*, 11 (1): 147-156.

Makeham, J. 2003. *New Confucianism: A Critical Examination*. Hampshire: Palgrave Macmillan.

Makin, P. 2005. Pound, Confucian sincerity, and America. *Paideuma*, 34 (2&3): 171-199.

Moody, A. D. 1982. *The Pisan Cantos*: Making cosmos in the wreckage of Europe. *Paideuma*, 11 (1): 135-146.

Morgan, G. 1942. Individualism versus individuality. *Ethics*, 52 (4): 434-446.

Nadel, I. B. 2010. *Ezra Pound in Context*. Cambridge: Cambridge University Press.

Nicol, E. 1949. Individuality and community. *Philosophy and Phenomenological Research*, 9 (3): 531-537.

Nolde, J. J. 1983. *Blossoms from the East: The China Cantos of Ezra Pound*. Orono: National Poetry Foundation, University of Maine.

Nolde, J. J. 1986. Ezra Pound and the "Ta Hio". *Paideuma*, 15 (2&3): 73-91.

Palandri, A. 1974. Homage to a Confucian poet. *Paideuma*, 3 (3): 301-311.

Pauthier, G. *Confucius et Mencius: Les Quatre Livres de Philosophie Morale et Politique de la Chine*. Paris: Charpentier, Libraire-Editeur, 1846.

Pound, E. 1950. *The Selected Letters of Ezra Pound: 1907-1941*. Ed. by D. D. Paige. New York: New Directions.Pound, E. 1968. *The Spirit of Romance*. New York: New Directions.

Pound, E. (Trans.) 1954. *Shih-ching: The Classic Anthology Defined by Confucius*. Cambridge: Harvard University Press.

Pound, E. (Trans.) 1969. *Confucius: The Unwobbling Pivot, The Great Digest and The Analects*. New York: New Directions.

Pound, E. 1970a. *Gaudier-Brzeska: A Memoir*. New York: New Directions.

Pound, E. 1970b. *Guide to Kulchur*. New York: New Directions.

Pound, E. 1970c. *Jefferson and/or Mussolini: L'idea Statale: Fascism as I Have Seen It*. New York: Liveright.

Pound, E. 1973. *Selected Poems of Ezra Pound*. Ed. by T. S. Eliot. London: Faber & Faber.

Pound, E. 1975a. *Pavannes and Divagations*. New York: New Directions.

Pound, E. 1975b. *Selected Prose, 1909-1965*. Ed. by W. Cookson. New York: New Directions.

Pound, E. 1976. *Collected Early Poems of Ezra Pound*. Ed. by M. J. King. New York: New Directions.

Pound, E. 1984. *Ezra Pound and Dorothy Shakespear: Their Letters 1909-1914*. Ed. by O. Pound and A. Walton Litz. New York: New Directions.

Pound, E. 1985. *Literary Essays of Ezra Pound*. Ed. by T. S. Eliot. London: Faber & Faber.

Pound, E. 1996a. *Machine Art and Other Writings: The Lost Thought of the Italian Years*. Ed. by M. L. Ardizzone. Durham: Duke University Press.

Pound, E. 1996b. *The Cantos of Ezra Pound*. New York: New Directions.

Pound, E. 1999. *Ezra and Dorothy Pound: Letters in Captivity, 1945-1946*. Ed. by O. Pound and R. Spoo. Oxford: Oxford University Press.

Qian, Z. M. 1995. *Orientalism and Modernism: The Legacy of China in Pound and Williams*. Durham: Duke University Press.

Qian, Z. M. 2003a. *Ezra Pound and China*. Ann Arbor: The University of Michigan Press.

Qian, Z. M. 2003b. *The Modernist Response to Chinese Art: Pound, Moore, Stevens*. Charlottesville and London: University of Virginia Press.

Qian, Z. M. 2006. Ezra Pound and his first Chinese contact for and against Confucianism. *Paideuma*, 35 (1&2): 157-177.

Qian, Z. M. 2008. *Ezra Pound's Chinese Friends: Stories in Letters*. New York: Oxford University Press.

Qian, Z. M. 2017. *East-West Exchange and Late Modernism — Williams, Moore, Pound*. Charlottesville and London: University of Virginia Press.

Redman, T. 1999. Pound's politics and economics. In I. B. Nadel (Ed.), *The Cambridge Companion to Ezra Pound* (pp. 249-263). Cambridge: Cambridge University Press.

Roger, T. A. & Peter, D. H. 2017. *Confucianism for a Changing World Cultural Order*. Honolulu: University of Hawaii Press.

Stead, C. K. 1986. *Pound, Yeats, Eliot and the Modernist Movement*. London: Macmillan.

Stock, N. 1961. Ezra Pound and the sense of responsibility. *Modern Age*, (1): 173-177.

Stock, N. 2011. *The Life of Ezra Pound*. London: Routledge.

Sun, H. 2003. Pound's quest for Confucian ideals: The Chinese history cantos. In Z. M. Qian (Ed.), *Ezra Pound and China* (pp. 96-119). Ann Arbor: University of Michigan Press.

Tan, X. C. 2014. Ezra Pound's conversion to Confucianism. *Journal of Literature and Art Studies*, 4 (3): 165-173.

Tay, W. S. 1977. *The Sun on the Silk: Ezra Pound and Confucianism* (Unpublished doctoral dissertation). University of California, San Diego.

Terrell, C. F. 1993. *A Companion to the Cantos of Ezra Pound*. 2 vols. Berkeley: University of California Press.

Torrey, E. F. 1999. *The Roots of Treason: Ezra Pound and the Secret of St. Elizabeths*. Bethesda: Lucas Publishers.

Tu, W. 1989. *Centrality and Commonality: An Essay on Confucian Religiousness*. Albany: State University of New York Press.

Wand, D. H. 1974. To the summit of Tai Shan: Ezra Pound's use of Chinese mythology. *Paideuma*, 3 (1): 3-12.

Witemeyer, H. 1969. *The Poetry of Ezra Pound: Forms and Renewal, 1908-1920*. Berkeley: University of California Press.

Xie, M. 1999. Pound as translator. In I. B. Nadel (Ed.), *The Cambridge Companion to Ezra Pound* (pp. 204-223). Cambridge: Cambridge University Press.

Yao, X. 1996. Self-construction and identity: The Confucian self in relation to some Western perceptions. *Asian Philosophy*, 6 (3): 179-195.

Zanotti, S. 2010. Fascism. In I. B. Nadel (Ed.), *Ezra Pound in Context* (pp. 376-391). Cambridge: Cambridge University Press.

Zhu, C. G. 2005. Ezra Pound's Confucianism. *Philosophy and Literature*, 29 (1): 57-72.

Zhu, C. G. 2006. Ezra Pound: The one-principle text. *Literature and Theology*, 20 (4): 394-410.